Broadway Christian C
Equipping for Missions A G
Bacon, Daniel W.

P9-DBT-578

0000   0278

equipping for
missions

by Daniel W. Bacon

equipping for missions

Copyright © 1992 OMF International

Published by Overseas Missionary Fellowship Inc.
10 W. Dry Creek Circle, Littleton, CO 80120

First printed 1992
This edition 2004

ISBN 1-929122-20-9

All rights reserved, including translation. No part of this
book may be reproduced or transmitted in any form or by
any means, electronic or mechanical, including photocopy-
ing, recording, or any information storage and retrieval system without written permission from OMF International,
2 Cluny Road, Singapore 259570, Republic of Singapore.
Printed in the United States of America.

Scripture taken from the
HOLY BIBLE NEW INTERNATIONAL VERSION®. NIV®.
Copyright ©1973, 1978, 1984 by International Bible Society.
Used by permission of Zondervan Publishing House.

OMF Books are distributed by
OMF, 10 West Dry Creek Circle, Littleton, CO 80120, USA
OMF, Station Approach, Borough Green, Sevenoaks, Kent
TN15 8BG, United Kingdom
OMF, PO Box 849, Epping, NSW 2121, Australia
OMF, 5155 Spectrum Way, Bldg. 21, Mississauga, ON L4W
5A1, Canada
OMF, PO Box 10159, Auckland, New Zealand
OMF, PO Box 3080, Pinegowrie 2123, South Africa
and other OMF offices.

equipping for missions

aligning your life
with the purpose of God

'll never forget my sense of anxiety. Had I really
missed the turnoff? Tumbling through my mind were
frantic thoughts of all the people who would be affected by my late arrival and the feeling of impending loss
of a great opportunity. Why had this happened to me?
Simply because I was lost in my own thoughts while
flying down the freeway, I'd missed the clearly marked
exit.

This scenario isn't uncommon. We all get lost occasionally in trying to navigate the complicated streets of
an unfamiliar neighborhood. While temporary incon-
venience is the usual outcome of losing our way, we can
be less concerned about our lives as Christians, where
the consequences of missing God's plan are much more
serious.

Someone has quipped, "If you know where you are
going, it makes it a lot easier to get there!" This is true

in the Christian life as well. The critical question we need to ask is, "What is the purpose or plan of God, and is my life aligned with that?"

What God is seeking to do in the world is very clear in Scripture. God has also emphasized how our individual lives need to conform to that grand design if we are to fulfill his divine destiny for us. Once you've made yourself available to God, to be part of what he is doing in this world through missions, it is vital to put specifics to your good intentions and to think through your plan for pursuing whatever purpose he has for you.

Unfortunately many Christians are engaged in an exercise of trivial pursuit.

- Every year thousands of young people make college plans without considering how they might best serve God's purpose in this world.
- Career decisions are made without adequate biblical input or awareness of the real needs and opportunities worldwide.
- In countless churches believers are busy, but unaware of the big picture and how their church fits into God's global plan.

How can we align our lives with God's best and highest purposes? Good choices come from good information. Let's see what Scripture says about God's purpose in this age and its implications. A solid biblical understanding of missions is vital if you are to stay on course.

THE PURPOSE OF GOD

It doesn't take long in reading Scripture to discover that God is a missionary God and that the Bible is a missionary book.

From Genesis to Revelation we see a God who is seeking his lost creation. We also discover that God has one main purpose that runs throughout the Bible. Although many of us have read the Old Testament in light of God's special love for Israel, in reality there are hundreds of references to God's purpose for all nations.

For example, look carefully at Psalm 96. What purposes for the nations are described in verses 7-9?

_____

_____

_____

In verses 3 and 10 what is God's purpose for Israel?

_____

_____

Now, let's see how God's missionary purpose runs throughout the Old Testament. You'll see: that God doesn't have several alternative tracks for those who reject his central purpose, nor is the Old Testament in opposition to the New. The God who loves the world in John 3:16 is the same God who reveals himself throughout the history of the Old Testament.

THE PLAN OF GOD

The first eleven chapters of Genesis are foundational to understanding the rest of the Bible. Here the stage is set for God's dealings with mankind. Man is created in the image of God, and his main role is to glorify God by exercising God's dominion over this planet (Gen. 1:27-28). However, man rebels against God's rule over him, and this results in spiritual and physical death entering the world and the human race (see Rom. 5:12). The good news is that God didn't abandon man or leave him to suffer the eternal consequences of his rebellion. The rest of the Bible is the story of God's reconciliation of alienated man and the outworking of his redemptive purpose.

Stage One: The Redemptive Plan Previewed

It's vital to see in Genesis 3:15 the outline for what God wants to do redemptively for mankind. This verse is often referred to as the "seed plot" of the Bible. What critical concepts do you see within it and how does it define the theme of the Bible?

_____

_____

In Genesis 3:15 we learn that God hasn't left man to die in his sins. Instead he promised a Savior and assured mankind that the outcome of the conflict between satanic forces and the purposes of God is not in doubt. This is the gospel in embryo.

Stage Two: The Redemptive Plan Advanced

Let's turn to another key passage to understand God's plan and methods of bringing redemption. Genesis 12:1-3 shows a step forward in the developing purpose and plan of God. What are the specific things God promises to accomplish through Abraham (Abram)?

I will _____ _____

(Through you) I will _____ _____ _____

In Genesis 1-11 God is dealing with mankind as a whole. Through the fall of man (Gen. 3), the flood (Gen. 6-8) and then the "flop" of the tower of Babel (Gen. 11), it is clear that mankind is on a collision course for self-destruction. But Genesis 12 introduces a change. Now God selects Abraham and promises to build a nation through him (Israel). Here we see the chosen instrument principle. God chooses a man to carry out his plan, but doesn't change his ultimate purpose.

How does Exodus 19:3-6 shed further light on God's purpose for choosing and using Israel?

_____

_____

Israel was called of God to fulfill a special role in the redemptive plan. God intended Israel to be a holy nation of royal priests (Exo. 19:3-6) that would mediate or represent the knowledge and character of God to all the nations around her. Isaiah 43:10 and Psalm 67:1-2 graphically describe Israel's special calling to be a witness and channel of blessing to the Gentiles. In using Abraham to create Israel as the people of God, the sovereign Lord never lost sight of the nations. In what practical ways was God's concern for Gentiles displayed in the following Old Testament passages?

Leviticus 19:33-34

_____

_____

1 Kings 8:41-43

_____

_____

1 Kings 17:7-24

_____

_____

Jonah 4

_____

_____

Isaiah 2:2-3

_____

While Israel had special privileges as the people of

God, they also had special missionary responsibilities. Instead of being sent on a missionary journey, Israel was to attract other nations by her godly and righteous living.

The God of Israel was not indifferent to the world but chose Israel as a channel through which all the nations could be blessed (Gen. 12:3). Even in the Old Testament God is revealed as the Creator, Lord and Judge of all the nations. He has never been provincial or narrow in his provisions, interests or activities. Far from being introduced for the first time in Matthew 28, missions has been in the purpose and plan of God from the start. The Old Testament not only contains missions but *is* missions.

God placed Israel at the most strategic geographic spot. Palestine was the crossroads of the world, a free-way interchange for three continents. As Israel fulfilled its covenant commitments and walked in obedience, blessing would come to all the nations.

At the same time, the Old Testament defines both the need and promise of a Savior. Israel was to be not only the recipient and guardian of God's special revelation to the world, but also the channel for the Messiah, who would provide redemption for all mankind (Gal. 4:5; Rom. 15:8-12; Isaiah 53).

Stage Three: The Redemptive Plan Fulfilled
As we come to the New Testament, we see right away

that it builds upon and consummates all that went before. Romans 15:8-9 states that Jesus Christ came to fulfill all the promises of God to Israel so that all Gentiles would benefit also. Let's look carefully at the mission of Christ in reference to both Israel and the world.

1. **His birth.** It was obvious from the beginning that God was sending Jesus for the entire world. What hints can you gain from the following Bible passages concerning God's universal intention?

   Matthew 2:1-12

   _____

   _____

   Luke 2:10, 14

   _____

   _____

   Luke 2:30-32

   _____

   _____

2. **His ministry.** Interestingly, almost one-third of Jesus' short-lived ministry was in Gentile areas. Much of his time was spent in Galilee (an area with a high population concentration of Gentiles) (Matt.

4:12-17). Throughout the Gospels, Jesus encounters Gentiles from time to time (Matt. 8:5-13), although his primary ministry was to the nation of Israel (Matt. 10:5-6).

3. **His teaching.** Sprinkled throughout the teachings of Jesus are references to a wider mission. While the term "Son of Man" has Messianic implications, it also suggests that Christ saw himself as the universal man and that his mission and message were for all. He conceived of his mission in worldwide terms, as seen in the frequent use of "the world" in John's Gospel. Jesus, furthermore, declared that the "field is the world" in the parable of the wheat and tares (Matt. 13:38). Surely he had more than geographic Palestine in mind. Finally Christ's own statement in John 10:16 explains that "other sheep" besides the flock of Israel were on his heart and in his divine mission.

4. **His death.** The New Testament writers boldly state that Christ's death was for all men, both Jew and Gentile alike. How do the following verses illustrate this?

1 John 2:2

_____

_____

2 Corinthians 5:14-21

_____

_____

_____

1 Timothy 2:5-6

_____

_____

_____

John 3:16-17

_____

_____

Stage Four: The Redemptive Plan Proclaimed
At the close of his ministry Jesus Christ gave his disciples and all who would follow them his Great Commission. Each Gospel account delivers that commission somewhat differently, and it is repeated again in Acts 1. Each expression helps us better understand the aim of the church's missionary mandate in fulfilling the purposes of God. What are some distinctive aspects of each account?

Matthew 28:18-20

_____

_____

Mark 16:15

_____

_____

Luke 24:44-49

_____

_____

John 20:21-23

_____

_____

Acts 1:8

_____

_____

In summary, throughout these great commission expressions our Lord stresses to his followers that:

1. **The gospel must be proclaimed to all nations.** The word nations comes from the Greek term _ethne,_ which actually refers to ethnic groups and not just to political states. As John puts it in Revelation 5:9, "... and with your blood you [Christ] purchased men for God from every tribe and language and people and nation."

2. **Forgiveness of sin in Christ's name must be offered to all.** Apart from Christ, men and women are eter-

nally lost and without hope (Acts 4:12). There is only one Savior and way to God (1 Tim. 2:5-6).

3. **Believers are to be established in congregations**, separated from old relationships by baptism, and instructed in the teachings of Christ to a new life of faith and obedience. This is all part of making disciples. Although there's no explicit command to "plant churches," in Acts we see that wherever the apostles proclaimed the gospel, local churches were the normal outcome.

4. **The power to obey the Great Commission comes ultimately from the Holy Spirit** (Acts 1:8). We haven't been given an impossible task nor a command we're unequipped to accomplish. The Great Commission remains Christ's command to his church today and is clearly our primary business until he returns.

5. **When Jesus issued the Great Commission, the whole church was in view**. His trailing remark in Matthew's account of the Commission, "And surely I am with you always, to the very end of the age..." clearly indicates that more than just the apostles were in view. Paul later writes to the church in Philippi to thank them for "...their partnership in the gospel from the first day until now..." (Phil. 1:5). With these verses in mind, what are some realistic ways in which every believer can participate in the Great Commission?

_____

_____

_____

_____

_____

THE WILL OF GOD FOR EVERY CHRISTIAN

What can we say about our personal response to Christ's commission? What does he expect? What should be our response? The following are some general statements applicable to each of us:

1. **Submission to the Lord of the Harvest** (Matt. 9:38)
    We begin by recognizing God's sovereignty over his work and our lives. We must grasp the simple but profound truth that God's work in this world is not a human enterprise which we are free to participate in or ignore as we please. But God, in answer to prayer, sends his people today into the harvest fields of the world, just as he sent Abraham, Jonah, Peter and Paul. Although the church has a crucial role in selecting, training, sending and supporting workers, it's still God's prerogative to place his servants in the field of his choice.

    What do you think happens when an individual refuses to do what God asks of him?

_____

_____

_____

_____

Before we can expect God's guidance, we need a submissive heart and a willingness to go wherever he directs. This is the tension point for most of us! We agree, but then quickly tack on our conditions like, "I'll go anywhere except where there are snakes, heat or restless natives!" Images of being boiled in a pot or carried away by army ants frightens some from even contemplating missions. Fears of perpetual singleness or separation from families are real emotions that condition our commitment and choke off any further inquiries. But Jesus' command is straightforward: "Whoever serves me must follow me; and where I am my servant will also be" (John 12:26). And with that directive Jesus adds the wonderful promise, "My Father will honor the one who serves me." Or, in the words of Hudson Taylor, the pioneer missionary to China who knew a great deal about personal sacrifice, "God gives the very best to those who leave the choice with him."

At this point, write an honest prayer about your fears and concerns regarding missionary service.

_____

_____

_____

_____

_____

_____

_____

2. Participation in the Great Commission now

The New Testament makes it clear that the Great Commission is the responsibility of the whole church. In this sense all of us are called to missions, and the church itself is called to be a missionary church. Every believer at the time of his or her salvation received a missionary call. That means that none of us is exempt, regardless of vocation. Obviously our plans for missionary work in the future should be an outgrowth of our participation in the Great Commission now. A plane trip doesn't make one a missionary. Several years ago, while talking with a seminary student about a church-planting ministry in Asia, I was shocked to discover that he had never led anyone to Christ. While spiritual gifts and God-given opportunities have a bearing, it's impossible to think that he was ready to evangelize Thai Buddhists when he had no experience in reaching those in his own community. In short, you should be involved as a world Christian and participating in ministry now, if you expect guidance for missionary work elsewhere someday.

What are you doing now to prepare yourself for service overseas?

_____

_____

_____

What steps can you take to become more involved?

_____

_____

_____

3. **Stewardship of potential**

   Stewardship in New Testament terms relates to all of life, not just in financial areas. What aspects of our lives (besides money) are we accountable for in the following passages?

   Matthew 25

   _____

   _____

   1 Peter 4:10

   _____

   _____

   Romans 12:2

   _____

   _____

2 Corinthians 5:9-10

_____

_____

The need to maximize potential and multiply our ministry is one guideline in assessing where to invest our time and energy. How should we use our resources?

Romans 12:3-8

_____

_____

2 Corinthians 9:6-11

_____

_____

There's a pattern in both Paul's ministry and the life of Christ, of working according to strategic needs and priorities (Rom. 15:20; Luke 15, 16). We can assume, then, that believers deciding where to invest their lives for God must consider where they can best use their gifts in obedience to the Great Commission. If, as a North American, I learn that ninety percent of the world's Christian workers serve only five percent of the earth's population in America, I should at least be open to serving in an area of greater need.

Based on God's desires for the world and Ephesians 5:15-17, what things should you consider in planning your vocation?

_____

_____

_____

_____

Perhaps part of the problem that leads to frequent inequality in the distribution of Christian workers is a distortion of the principle that a Christian can serve God anywhere. While true, it doesn't mean all vocations or locations are of equal priority and value, though all are of equal significance if we are in the work God has chosen for us. Not every vocation is equally strategic in building the church worldwide. For this reason Paul in 1 Corinthians 12:28 gives priority to the gifts that spread the gospel to unreached areas in order to plant the church. As a Christian, then, you need to take an honest, hard look at where you invest your gifts, rather than just taking the line of least resistance or the nearest opportunity.

Take a minute to evaluate how your current vocational plans may or may not fit in with God's purpose and plan for the world.

_____

_____

_____

_____

_____

_____

Well, we've covered a lot in this first lesson, but a solid foundation is essential if the rest of the building is to stand firm and function effectively. Remember that this course is designed to help you prepare for involvement in world missions even if you never become a career missionary. Actually going cross-culturally is only one response of obedience to the Great Commission.

In the following chapters I'd like to provide a road map to help you grow in your commitment to global missions, and find concrete ways to explore options, make wise choices, and discern your potential contribution.

Here are some other resources on the topic of the biblical theology of missions you might want to check out for additional material:

A People for His Name by Paul A. Beals, Baker Book House, 1988.

Christian Missions in Biblical Perspective by J. Herbert Kane, Baker Book House, 1976.

The Great Omission by Robertson McQuilkin, Baker Book House, 1984.

A Biblical Theology of Missions by George W. Peters, Zondervan, 1970.

Let the Nations Be Glad! The Supremacy of God in Mission by John Piper, Baker Book House, 1993.

2

putting things into perspective

A quick glance at our world today proves the Great Commission has been taken seriously by the church. The church has become a worldwide movement claiming nearly one-third of humanity as professing Christians.

In this lesson we want to first get an overview of the expansion of the church from its inception in the first century. Next, we'll watch some critical developments in the history of missions and learn some of its important lessons. Finally, for our challenge and encouragement, we'll introduce some influential missionaries you need to know as models and examples. Many of their methods are still used today.

THE MISSIONARY EXPANSION OF THE CHURCH
Winning the Empire. A.D. 30-500

Missions began in the Book of Acts. A handful of apostles, empowered by the resurrected Christ, moved out in dynamic witness to a hostile world. There's no human explanation as to why Christianity should survive, let alone thrive to become a worldwide phenomena. But the key is found in Acts 1:8. What is it?

_____

_____

After Pentecost, Christianity began to spread throughout the Roman Empire. While the apostles accounted for some of that growth, what other factors accelerated the missionary movement?

Acts 8: 1-4

_____

_____

Acts 11: 19-21

_____

_____

Paul, Silas, Barnabas and Peter led the way in early evangelism and were joined by lay Christians everywhere in spreading the good news of Christ. At the close of Paul's ministry, there is evidence of churches spreading from Jerusalem to southern Yugoslavia (Rom. 15:19).

The church, which began as a tiny, persecuted

minority of 120 disciples in Acts 1, had become the official religion of the empire by the end of the 4th century. The German scholar Harnack calculates that there were about 30,000 Christians in Rome by 250 A.D. It is estimated that as much as ten percent of the Roman Empire's population were Christians by 313. The amazing spread of the church continued from the Middle East to North Africa, parts of Europe, eastward into Mesopotamia and beyond in the first four centuries of her existence. Dr. Herbert Kane highlights some reasons for this rapid growth:

1. Roman rule provided a superb network of roads, relative political stability and peaceful conditions to help the spread of the gospel.
2. Greek was the trade language of the Empire and helped to facilitate communication. The Bible was also available in Greek.
3. Jewish communities scattered throughout the Empire provided natural bridges to Gentile people. They became a a foothold for ministry into the pagan world and accelerated the growth of the church.
4. The quality of Christians' lives in the midst of moral and philosophical bankruptcy gave credence to the message of the gospel. Even when persecuted, the early church was a bright light to the lost and disillusioned in a very dark age.
5. Following the conversion of Emperor Constantine in 313, the Roman government supported Christianity.

This endorsement was a mixed blessing, but brought Christianity to the people of the Empire.[1]

What are some factors in today's world that can hasten the spreading of the gospel abroad?

_____

_____

_____

Can you see yourself serving in connection with any of these? How?

_____

_____

_____

The Christianization of Europe. A.D. 500-1200
Over the next centuries the church faced three formidable challenges: the peril of state religions; reaching the Barbarians; and the rise of Islam. This period is now characterized as the dark ages, but not all was dark.

1. **The peril of state religion.** The legalization of Christianity in 313 by the Roman emperor Constantine's Edict of Milan gave religious freedom to all. The church found a friend and supporter in the state, whereas previously there had been bitter enmity. Christians suddenly found themselves in favored and prestigious positions. Emperor

Constantine became a supporter of Christianity, and offered political power to the church.

In the merger of church and state the church shifted from its original dynamic and became a social institution. Professional clergy replaced the laity as keys to the growth and ministry of the church. Churches acquired land and built buildings, which enhanced their sense of power. The church became the wealthiest institution of that day. As the Holy Roman Empire grew, the church became paganized and secularized and thus lost its spiritual power and authority.

2. **Reaching the Barbarians.** Missions took a new direction as the Roman Empire was Christianized. To the north of Rome the Goths, Visigoths and Vikings threatened to strike. As the church grew more closely allied with the state, Christianity was often used to foster imperial expansion. The besieged Empire viewed missions politically, and hoped evangelistic efforts would help to bring outlying areas under Roman control.

Sometimes when kings and other rulers were converted, group baptisms resulted. For example, Clovis, king of the Franks, was converted in 496 following an unexpected military victory. Seeing the victory as a sign from God, he celebrated by being baptized along with 3,000 of his troops. These mass conversions became common during the Middle Ages and account for much of the Christianization of Europe.

There were also marvelous examples of men who sincerely sought to proclaim Christ to the heathen. Patrick is a prime example. Born in a Christian home in Britain around 389, he was carried off to Ireland by marauders as a young teen. During his captivity he came to a deep faith in Christ. Once freed, he eventually returned to Ireland and became a fiery evangelist. Through his efforts the Celtic church became a bastion for missions. From Ireland missionaries evangelized Britain and major parts of Western Europe. Other missionaries such as Ulfilas, Columba, Boniface, Augustine and Anskar had major roles in carrying the gospel to Europe.

On a different front, the Nestorian movement spearheaded the spread of the gospel to Asia and China. According to historian John Stewart, the Nestorian church was the most missionary church the world has ever seen. As part of the Eastern church, the Nestorians moved into China by the 9th century and then to Korea, Japan and Southeast Asia. They were considered heretics by Roman Catholics, but more objective assessments show doctrinal issues were over-stressed and their contribution to missions is of tremendous significance.

What are some advantages and disadvantages of a state religion?

_____

_____

3. **Confronting Islam.** The emergence of Islam in the 7th century was a major watershed in the history of Christianity. The church faced a new and formidable enemy which had the strength of religious conviction backed by racial pride. As Islam swept across North Africa, it quickly encountered established Christianity. Sadly, the church caved into the pressure and was almost totally absorbed into Islamic culture. Without the historic Battle of Tours in Southern France in 732, when Islamic forces were stopped by the armies of Charles Martel, the face of Europe could have changed forever.

Unfortunately, Christianity later responded with military retaliation and hate, rather than with love and evangelism. The Crusades (1095-1291) were one of the greatest tragedies in the history of the church and have severely hindered subsequent authentic efforts to lovingly share the gospel with Muslims.

If you were Muslim, how might this historical background affect your perception of Christianity? Use your answer in praying for evangelism efforts throughout the Muslim world.

_____

_____

_____

_____

_____

Roman Catholic Missions. A.D. 1300-1700

Christianity probably wouldn't have become a truly international faith without the tremendous efforts of the missionary orders in the Catholic church. They played key roles in the spread of the church when much of Christendom was heavily involved in local ecclesiastical and political affairs rather than world evangelism. Missionaries of these special orders were responsible for planting the church in Asia, Africa and Latin America.

The oldest of these orders is the Benedictines, founded in the 6th century. The Augustinians, Franciscans and Dominicans didn't surface until the 13th century. Finally the Jesuits were founded in the 16th century by Ignatius of Loyola.

The Jesuits became the most aggressive and dominant force in the advance of Roman Catholic missions. Outstanding individuals served in these orders. Francis Xavier in Japan, Matteo Ricci in India and Robert de Nobili of India number among them. Their efforts are worthy of our admiration and imitation.

Early Protestant Missions. A.D. 1600-1800

While the Protestant Reformation brought much needed correction to the church's doctrine and practice, it unfortunately did not lead to a fresh outpouring of missionary interest, at least initially. The new understanding of salvation by grace through faith alone, the availability of the Scriptures to all believers and the excitement of new-found freedom quickly lost its impact by political and doctrinal infighting among Protestant groups. While Protestantism demonstrated little missionary zeal, the Catholic church gained in global outreach what it had lost in Reformation Europe. Herbert Kane lists several factors which contributed to the lack of mission vision among Protestant churches.

1. The Reformers taught that the Great Commission applied only to the original apostles who fulfilled it in their day. If later generations were without the gospel, it was their own fault and the church should not intervene.

2. While the Catholic church launched a successful counter-reformation, the Lutheran and Reformation churches fought doctrinal and organizational battles among themselves, thus diverting potential interest away from missions.

3. Protestant Europe (northern) was more geographically isolated from Asia, Africa and the New World. Long before the Reformation, Catholic missions were involved in worldwide travel, and already had

experience and vision, as well as experienced sailors and ships.

4. Protestant churches had no religious orders committed exclusively to the cause of missions. The Jesuits and Franciscans were organized specifically to spread Catholicism effectively around the world.[2]

Do you see any of these issues remaining in the church today? What might be done to correct them?

_____

_____

_____

_____

Nonetheless, God was quietly at work behind the scenes preparing individuals to spark a new surge of missionary effort by Protestants. Look at some of the noteworthy players in this unfolding drama:

1. **The Pietists.** Modern missions grew out of the Pietist movement of Germany. They revolted against the barren orthodoxy and formalism that had settled into Protestantism. Philip Spencer and August Francke emphasized a personal conversion experience, Bible study, prayer and evangelistic zeal. The Danish-Halle Mission sent their first missionaries to India in 1705, which became a prototype of pioneer missionary work.

2. **The Moravians.** Moravian missions is an amazing

34

story of commitment, sacrificial service and obedience to the Great Commission. A Moravian colony in Germany, led by Count Nicholas Zinzendorf, launched a missionary movement unparalleled in history. In 1732 their first missionaries went to the Virgin Islands and Greenland. By 1760 some 226 Moravian missionaries entered ten foreign countries. The proportion of field missionaries to members at home was an incredible 1:60. The overseas congregation was three times as large as the European sending church.

3. **William Carey.** A water-shed experience for Protestant missions occurred when William Carey left England in 1792 and sailed to India. His example inspired many new mission agencies and individuals. Remember him as "the father of modern missions."

4. **The Haystack Movement.** God used several students to ignite interest in missions in America, as had been used in Europe. Samuel Mills and a group of students committed themselves to pray for world needs. They often met in a grove of trees for discussion and prayer. One day a sudden thunderstorm sent them for refuge in a nearby haystack. Under this cover, they prayed for the unreached peoples of the world and resolved to become America's first foreign missionaries. From this modest beginning, the American Board of Commissioners for Foreign

Missions was inaugurated, and soon sent Adoniram Judson with others to India and Burma in 1812. A steady stream of missionaries followed.

The Great Century of Missions. A.D. 1800–present
By the mid-1800s interest in world missions was touching many lives. Technology plus a deepened desire for colonial expansion fueled awareness of the peoples of Africa and Asia. Historian Kenneth Latourette termed the 19th century "The Great Century" for missions. Protestant missions expanded at its highest rate since the church began. You should be familiar with the following strategic developments:

1. **The growth of faith missions.** When Hudson Taylor went to China in 1853, little did he know how God would use him or the organization he later founded, the China Inland Mission. He's been called "the father of faith missions." The CIM, founded in 1865 and today known as OMF International, set a pattern for many similar agencies spawned in the later 19th century and 20th century. Some continue today. Faith missions became the channel for thousands of committed Christians' pioneering work in most countries. Many of these organizations are part of the Interdenominational Foreign Missions Association, whose member missions total about 7,000 missionaries.

2. **The Bible societies.** Special mention should be

made of the Bible societies, which have been extremely valuable to the missions movement. Pioneers in the field were the British and Foreign Bible Society (1804), the National Bible Society of Scotland (1809), the Netherlands Bible Society (1814), and the American Bible Society (1816). These societies, with their national counterparts in other places, vastly increased the availability of the Word of God over the past 150 years. Missionaries have done an incredible job translating Scriptures which have been published by these societies.

3. **The Student Volunteer Movement.** In the late 1880s, through the influence of D. L. Moody, an organization launched the mobilization of North American and European students into world missions. Through the missionary vision of Robert Wilder, and later the organizational genius of John R. Mott, the Student Volunteer Movement for Foreign Missions was instrumental in sending 20,500 students abroad in 50 years' time. The entire church was impacted by their involvement.

4. **The Bible Institute Movement.** Also in the late 1880s D. L. Moody's desire to train Christian workers added numerous Bible schools to the growing missionary movement. Schools like Moody Bible Institute (1886) produced the majority of candidates for the faith missions and were part of God's program to stir the church to fulfill its missions responsibility.

Terry Hulbert summarizes the 19th century as one of initiative and penetration by missions, and the first half of the 20th century as a period of consolidation. Most major areas of the world have at least been touched by the gospel. Today we need to expand these footholds through new churches and evangelizing the thousands of unreached people groups.[3]

We've seen that God has used may different individuals and events in the history of missions. Write a prayer to the Lord of the harvest to inquire how he would like to use you to impact your world for him.

_____

_____

_____

What is one way you feel God can use you?

_____

_____

To read more about mission history, I suggest *A Concise History of the Christian World Mission* by Herbert Kane, Baker Book House, 1973) or the classic by Stephen Neil, *A History of Christian Missions* (Penguin, 1964).

1 J. Herbert Kane, *A Concise History of the Christian World Mission*, Baker, 1973, p. 6.
2 *Ibid*, p. 73.
3 Hulbert, Terry C. *World Missions Today*, Evangelical Teacher Training Association, Wheaton, 1979, p.29.

Knowing the game plan

I t has been said that the mission fields of the world are littered with the wreckage of good intentions. After my 35 years of missionary service, I can certainly agree with that. Maybe it will help us first to look at a New Testament model of the church in action and see its strategy and priorities.

In Acts we're introduced to the Antioch church. This church is a dynamic model of a missionary church. What God did in Antioch, I believe, he wants to do in a thousand other places. Antioch became the home base for a worldwide mission enterprise. This church is first described in Acts 11:19-30. Identify some of the major activities of this group.

_____

_____

_____

_____

Next, Acts 13:1-2 shows a fresh challenge laid on this body of believers. What was this?

_____

_____

_____

_____

How did they respond to Paul and Barnabas in 13:3?

_____

_____

_____

Paul and his companion Barnabas obeyed God's call and left for their first missionary journey. In chapters 13 and 14 we see them traveling from place to place, and then returning to Antioch in Acts 14:26. In reviewing their missionary journey, can you see any evidence of their strategy or goals?

13:5, 14-16, 42-44, 14:1, where did they preach?

_____

_____

14: 1-7 _____

_____

A similar pattern emerges from Acts 15:36 onwards as

Paul and his apostolic band continue to travel and preach. Wherever the apostles went to evangelize, the outcome was always making disciples and planting churches. We can summarize the strategy of Paul's ministry in the following outline by Herbert Kane:

1. Paul concentrated on large metropolitan centers— e.g. Philippi, Ephesus, Athens, and Rome.

2. He confined his initial efforts to four eastern provinces in the empire (Galatia, Asia, Macedonia and Achaia) and later on Western Europe. There are apparently three major movements in his over-all strategy: (1) starting from Antioch in the eastern Mediterranean, (2) shift HQ to Ephesus to evangelize Asia Minor and Greece, and (3) shift HQ to Rome to evangelize Western Europe.

3. He worked in close cooperation with his home church—Antioch (Acts 13:1-3; 14:27-28; 18:22). He also touched base with the mother church in Jerusalem, making numerous visits to that city (Acts 9:26; 11:27-30; 15:2; 21:17).

4. He followed the principle "to the Jew first" (Acts 13:13-46; Rom 1:16). Only when the Jews rejected the message did he turn to Gentiles (Acts 18:6). It's interesting to consider whether this was primarily for theological or strategic reasons, or perhaps even both.

5. Paul made the synagogue the scene of his chief labors. The strategic value of this was that the syn-

agogue became a bridge into the Gentile community (Acts13:46-48; 14:1; 17:1-4; 18:4).

6. He remained in one place as long as he could: Thessalonica—3 weeks (Acts 17:2).
Corinth—18 months (Acts 18:11).
Ephesus—3 years (Acts 20:31).

7. He supported himself and his colleagues by tent making at times (Acts 20:34; 1 Thess. 2:9). He was also grateful for support gifts from churches (Phil. 4:14-19).

8. He carefully instructed and nurtured young converts in biblical truths (Acts 18:23; 20:20-31; Col. 1:28; 1 Thess. 2:11).

9. He gathered his converts into churches (Acts 14:23). Paul expected these churches to become self-supporting (1 Cor. 16:1-2); self-governing (1 Cor. 5:4-5); and self-propagating (1 Thess. 1:7-8).

10. Paul was strong in convictions and principles but flexible in his methods or approaches (1 Cor. 9:20-22).

11. Though his essential message was always the same, he adapted its presentation to the audience needs.[1]

To biblically oriented Jews in Antioch in Acts 13, what did Paul assume and what was his message?

_____

_____

_____

_____

In Acts 14:8-20, how did Paul adapt his message to communicate with primitive animists?

_____

_____

_____

_____

What adjustment did Paul make to better reach the educated urbanites in Acts 17:16-31?

_____

_____

_____

_____

12. He made good use of fellow workers and delegated tasks.
    First Journey—Barnabas and Mark (Acts 13:2).
    Second Journey—Silas, Timothy and Luke (Acts 15:40; 16:3; 16:11).
    Third Journey—Luke, Timothy, Gaius and others (Acts 20:4).

13. Paul did not allow persecution to deter him (Acts 14:22; 21:13), yet he did not court danger in an unreasonable or foolhardy way (Acts 9:23-24).

14. He prayed constantly for his converts and nur-

tured them with follow-up letters (Eph. 1:16; Phil. 1:3-4; Col. 1:9, 2:1).

15. He employed miracles to authenticate his message (Acts 13:9-12; 19:11-12; Rom. 15:19).

If you were planning to work as a missionary to an unreached people group, how might these principles shape your strategy or approach?

_____

_____

_____

_____

DEFINING THE TASK

Even from this cursory examination, we can see that the task of missions involves strategy. While we do not have evidence of Paul's use of a detailed statement of purpose, objectives, goals and standards common to our contemporary management language, Scripture makes it clear that he wasn't aimless or haphazard in planning and carrying out his ministry. Neither can our missionary outreach afford to be careless if we are to see effective church-planting movements or accomplish our biblical mandate of discipling the nations. If God is leading you into missions, you must thoroughly understand the job to be done.

Let's summarize the mission of the church with the commands of Christ (Matt.28:19-20) and Paul's example:

44

Preaching—proclamation of the gospel by all possible means.

Teaching—Edifying believers and making disciples.

Planting—Establishing new believers in churches.

Perfecting—Stimulating growth and maturity.

In the above task is the fundamental assumption that without the gospel people are eternally lost. Recently an old, insidious heresy raised its ugly head, threatening missions in some circles: the doctrine of universalism, which denies that without saving faith in Jesus Christ, men are eternally lost and separated from God. Just as the ancient Trojan horse deceived the citizens, leading to the defeat of the city, so today neo-universalism infiltrates and influences the evangelical church, leading to the loss of our vision and the abandonment of our mission.

Admittedly, the thought of an eternal hell is far from pleasant, but the important issue is not, "do we like this teaching," but rather, "what does the Bible teach about this matter?" Check out these passages:

Matthew 13:49-50

_____

_____

Matthew 25:41

_____

_____

2 Thessalonians1 :8-9

_____

_____

Revelation 20:13-15

_____

_____

The Bible clearly teaches that there are only two destinies open to man. The lostness of man is a forceful fact of Scripture, and one we must take seriously in order to remain loyal to Scripture and the teachings of Jesus Christ. Any confusion over this primary issue cuts the nerve of missions and paralyzes the church's outreach.

In terms of motivation for missions, however, it is important to keep in view that what is at stake is not just man's eternal destiny or the needs of the world. As John Piper has put it in his outstanding book, _Let the Nations Be Glad! The Supremacy of God in Missions_:

Missions is not the ultimate goal of the church. Worship is. Missions exist because worship doesn't. Worship is ultimate, not missions, because God is ultimate, not man. When this age is over, and the countless millions of the redeemed fall on their faces before the throne of God, missions will be no more. It is a temporary necessity. But worship abides forever.

In other words, our ultimate motivation in missions

is not to seek only the welfare and benefits of salvation for men, but that God may receive the honor, glory and worship he alone deserves from the nations (Psalm 96).

Defining the "mission" of the church in recent years has not been easy. A major debate has emerged as to what the church is and what the church is supposed to be doing. From a biblical perspective, however, the church may have many responsibilities but only one mission, and that is the evangelization and discipling of all nations. The goal of evangelism is to persuade men and women to become disciples of Christ and responsible members of his church.

But what about other responsibilities the church has to our society and to the world? Are we to be concerned only with people's souls and not their bodies? What about injustice which wounds the spirit, or the deep poverty which starves children in so many places? To answer these important questions, we'll discuss two scriptural mandates:

1. **The Cultural Mandate.** In Genesis God commanded Adam, "Be fruitful and increase in number; fill the earth and subdue it. Rule over the fish of the seas and the birds of the air and over every living creature that moves on the ground" (Gen. 1:28). After God formed man, he "put him in the Garden of Eden to work it and take care of it" (Gen. 2:15). Following the flood, God gave the same mandate to

Noah (Gen. 9:1, 7). In short, the cultural mandate applies to every person, Christian or otherwise, and expresses God's intention for the exploration, development and improvement of man's social structures and physical environment. It is man's responsibility to build a wholesome culture in which he can live as a true human being according to the moral order and creative purposes of God. It is also his responsibility to exercise good stewardship of natural resources entrusted to him for the benefit of mankind.

2. **The Redemptive Mandate.** This mandate is often referred to as the Great Commission or evangelistic mandate. It mostly relates to the church and sets priorities for the Christian's unique responsibility to the world—to proclaim the gospel and disciple the nations.

How then do we relate to the two mandates as Christians and as a church? Jesus said believers are to serve as both "salt and light" in this world (Matt. 5:13-16). Paul encouraged Christians to not become weary in well doing, but as we have opportunity, "let us do good to all people, especially to those who belong to the family of believers" (Gal. 6:10). Therefore, both mandates relate to us yet should be kept in balance and perspective.

Some polarize these activities into mutually

exclusive categories: evangelism versus social action. Others see them as parallel activities which are both biblically motivated and equal in value, but distinct activities. Still others prioritize these tasks, stressing the spiritual over the cultural but each contributing to the Kingdom of God. Perhaps any false dichotomy can be avoided by stressing the biblical primacy of evangelism as the unique task of the church, yet acknowledging the need for good works to accompany the proclamation of the gospel. Wholesome social action should result or be an outcome once the gospel is believed and obeyed.

QUESTIONS FOR THOUGHT AND DISCUSSION

In your local situation, what do you think are your church's social and/or political responsibilities? Is there a distinction between those responsibilities which belong to individual believers, and those which relate to the church as a whole?

_____

_____

_____

_____

In summarizing this section on mission strategy, it's helpful to outline the critical questions that need to be asked and answered to make sure we stay on track. Peter Wagner gives us a useful framework for develop-

ing a strategy to reach the people groups of this world
with the gospel:

> *The right goals*
> *The right place*
> *The right time*
> *The right personnel*
> *The right methods* [2]

1. **The Right Goals.** We have already commented at
   length about the task of missions. But it might be
   helpful to expand our understanding of the evangelistic mission of the church using the following
   steps:

   Presence. Presence evangelism means influencing
   by the lifestyle of the believer in word, deed and
   attitude. It is reflected in care for people and acts
   of love. In itself presence evangelism may not
   include verbal witness, but demonstrates the love
   of Christ for people in need. For instance,
   Christian medical work, community development
   projects or refugee aid may all be aspects of
   Christian presence.

   Proclamation. The church is called to preach the
   good news of Christ. There's no substitute for verbal proclamation, but the message must be vali-
   dated by quality Christian living.

   Persuasion. To produce results, proclamation must
   seek to bring a positive response to the message.

Jesus called men and women to a decision concerning himself, and so must we. The purpose of evangelism is to make disciples.

Planting. It isn't enough to make isolated disciples. The pattern in Scripture congregates Christians in local churches for their edification and encouragement. Church planting is the primary goal of evangelism.

Propagation. Evangelization aims at planting churches that will plant other churches and thus spread the gospel to their own people and beyond.

2. **The Right Place.** When you think of Christ's words to make disciples of all nations what comes to mind? Do you see "nations" as just the geographic countries of the United Nations? This is understandable, but realize the word nations in Matthew 28:19 is the Greek word *ethne,* which actually means ethnic or people groups. The recent battles between ethnic groups in Eastern Europe and the former Soviet Union highlight this distinction. One *country* (political) can contain many *nations* (socio-ethno-linguistic peoples). It's a staggering fact that while there are churches in almost every country, estimates say some 11,000 people groups remain unevangelized. Some of these groups are tribal, while others represent major language and cultural groups that are

Muslim, Hindu and Buddhist. Some may also be social enclaves in large cities.

In thinking of world evangelization, the first question we ask is what peoples are still in need of the gospel and how do we locate them? The problem is we've often focused solely on geography in locating unreached people rather than including important cultural considerations. The Lausanne Committee for World Evangelization and others have come up with the following operational definition to help identify the unreached and define our strategies:

From the viewpoint of evangelization, a people group is the largest group within which the gospel can spread as a church-planting movement without encountering barriers of acceptance and understanding.

The next chapter will show our main task is to discover the people groups of our world still without a witness or churches strong enough to evangelize their own people, and to prioritize them for evangelization.

3. **The Right Time.** The Apostle Paul in Acts 17:26-27 speaks of God as not only the Creator of all nations, but also as sovereignly at work in their histories, that "...men would seek him and perhaps reach out for him and find him..."—meaning that behind our efforts towards world evangelization is the work of

God to prepare people for the gospel. We should realize that not all peoples are equally ready for the message at any given time. Jesus himself spoke of harvests that are ripe (Matt. 9:37-38).

Stages of preparation may be required before resistant peoples become receptive. While receptive people should have a certain priority, we cannot and should not neglect those who remain resistant. Sometimes peoples thought to be resistant simply have never heard the gospel in a thoughtful, culturally appropriate way. Through prayer, careful preparation and the sovereign activity of God, resistance will be overcome and the harvest will be ripe. God promises that the right time will come for each people to hear the gospel and respond. Our responsibility is to go, to learn to love the people and sensitively communicate with them. We must seek to enter and engage every group possible, and constantly test the soil so that when the harvest is prepared, the workers will be ready also. When the time is right, God will send the harvest.

Think through political and social developments in China since 1949. How have these helped or hindered the growth of the church there?

_____

_____

_____

Assignment: Read *Eternity in Their Hearts* by Don Richardson for a helpful grasp of how God works through culture and historical circumstances.

4. **The Right Personnel.** Many churches are coming alive to the needs and opportunities for world evangelization like never before. Some are focusing on particular unreached people groups for special prayer and the sending of mission teams. The Adopt-A-People movement expresses this approach and is very commendable. Others see the national church of a given country as a logical instrument for evangelism and recognize the need to financially support national workers. Many churches believe that they can best accomplish God's purposes by providing resources to mission agencies who serve as their partners in world evangelization. Some have determined that since the church now exists in every country, all missionaries should be brought home, and the national church given sole responsibility for evangelization.

It is critical to remember that the forces for evangelization include both the church at home and the national church on the field. Every effort should be made to foster cooperation in outreach and share resources where appropriate. However, not every national church is in a position to effectively reach out cross-culturally. Many lack the vision to do so. Others may lack the resources or training. Sometimes it is just a matter of relative immaturity that prevents effective outreach. Sometimes because of racial/ethnic tensions or prior hostility between peoples geographically near but culturally antagonistic, someone from outside both groups may need to take the first steps to communicate the gospel. Therefore, it is both necessary and appropriate for mission efforts to come in from outside and work cross-culturally to evangelize a group. With so many groups remaining to be evangelized, every effort must be made to reach these peoples without unnecessary duplication.

Respond to the statement, "It's less costly and more efficient to support nationals rather than missionaries."

_____

_____

_____

_____

_____

5. **The Right Methods.** Thus far we've talked about the mission task and tried to define it carefully.

We've looked at our scriptural goals, how to view the unreached world as people groups, the issue of receptivity, and the forces available for evangelization. There is one last consideration: the issue of choosing the right methods. Not every approach is biblically valid or culturally effective. If we're to have God's blessing, our work must be done in God's way.

It's essential that our methods be biblically based. Does that mean we must precisely duplicate Paul's methods? Is there a uniform method that's universally applicable?

A quick look at Scripture and a review of Paul's methodology demonstrates that while methods must vary, some principles always apply. Furthermore, methods must be sensitive to the culture of the people group, and communication must be appropriate. Stewardship of time, funds and personnel are important factors in choosing the best methods. In the end we realize that ultimately the work is God's and not ours. We must prayerfully plan, but only God can produce the harvest.

List some specific elements you'd like to see worked into your church's missions strategy.

_____

_____

_____

_____

_____

_____

How can you help bring that about?

_____

_____

_____

For further study, I recommend the following resource tools:

Beals, Paul A., *A People for His Name: A Church Based Missions Strategy*. Baker Book House, 1988.

Kane, J. Herbert, *Understanding Christian Missions*. Baker Book House, 1982.

Peters, George, *A Biblical Theology of Missions*. Moody Press, 1972.

Piper, John, *Let the Nations Be Glad! The Supremacy of God in Missions*. Baker Book House, 1993.

Wagner, C. Peter. *On The Crest of the Wave: Becoming a World Christian*. Regal Books, 1983.

Winter and Hawthorne. *Perspectives on the World Christian Movement; A Reader*. William Carey Library, 1981, 1992, 1999.

1 J. Herbert Kane, *Christian Missions in a Biblical Perspective*, Baker, 1976, pp. 73-85.

2 *Perspectives on the World Christian Movement: A Reader*, Edited by Ralph Winter and Stephen Hawthorne, p. 573.

sensing
the scene

What in the world is happening? In many ways things look as if they're falling apart and fast. On the other hand, the church of Jesus Christ in the 21st century has made phenomenal progress. As Stan Guthrie puts it, "The fruit of the worldwide evangelistic task is unmistakably impressive. A third of the world's people call themselves Christians. Christianity in all its forms has become the world's most global faith. Followers of Jesus are present in every country. Countless lives have been transformed by the risen and reigning Christ, especially in the 20th century." That's a significant claim and bears closer scrutiny. But let's back up a minute to sense something of the context in which we're being called to disciple the nations in today's world. What's really happening? Where should we be going?

There's no doubt that God is doing amazing things

in our days. Unfortunately a lot of it doesn't make the local newspaper, or even warrant mention from our pulpits. We're often so focused on the immediate around us that we have no idea what the wider picture is. But from God's perspective, headlines are being made daily. To be a part of what he is doing in this world is the most exciting and challenging task there is.

CHURCH GROWTH WORLDWIDE

Regarding the challenge of the Great Commission, evangelical church and mission leaders have every reason to be optimistic. That optimism is founded ultimately not on our skills and strategies but on Christ's promise to build his church (Matthew 16:18), and the prophetic picture of believers from all tribes, languages and nations vividly displayed in Revelation 5:9. That doesn't imply indifference to the harsh realities of persecution of Christians in many places, the growth of major non-Christian religions such as Islam, rejection of the gospel by secular humanists, erosion of moral values in the West, and other forms of opposition. Nor do we naively hope all will become Christians in our world. Instead it states a confidence that God is at work galvanizing fresh efforts in his church to complete his task in his power. Just look at what God has done in recent decades:

Africa was once known as the Dark Continent by Christians. In 1900 the Christian population was only

10 percent, but now is over 40 percent, at least nominally Christian and growing phenomenally. In Latin America the evangelical movement is growing three times as fast as the population and now numbers close to 50 million people. Brazil has seen some of the greatest church growth reported anywhere in the world. Europe has changed dramatically in recent years with significant church growth in the former USSR and other eastern European countries. Even traditionally resistant Muslim areas are showing new signs of interest in the gospel with significant church growth in Indonesia and parts of North Africa.

In spite of cultural and religious obstacles, even the church in Asia has grown dramatically recently. A century ago there were only a handful of churches in Korea; yet today over 2,000 churches interlace the streets of Seoul. Forty years ago the church in China was a tiny island in a sea of humanity. Despite radical opposition, the church has exploded with upwards of 50 million believers. Similar stories of growth and advance could be told of East Malaysia, Indonesia, Mongolia and the Philippines. Truly, our God hasn't called us to an impossible task.

The resources for evangelizing the world have likewise increased in these days. According to Dr. Ralph Winter, some 350 new mission agencies have been established since 1950 in the U.S. alone. More significantly, a similar number have come into being in the so-called Third World so that there are some 103,000 missionaries from these areas in addition to the 100,000 from traditional Western sending countries. Furthermore, in our generation we've seen rapid technological development of all kinds of tools to help us do our job better and faster—media tools such as the Jesus Film, radio broadcasts in over 565 languages, audio cassettes in some 5,000 languages to present the gospel to people without a written language, and Bible portions translated into more than 2,500 languages with the aid of computers. The use of the internet for evangelism and discipling has also become a widely used tool.

NEEDS AND OPPORTUNITIES

With all this marvelous growth, who needs more missionaries? Is the need for more missionaries real and factual or just the meaningless chatter of a missionary enterprise unable to come to grips with the fact that its time has come—and gone? Hardly! A casual look at our world through spiritual eyes will confirm immediately that the need for more missionaries is anything but a myth. Let's look at the other side of the world to back this up.

In our world of 6.1 billion people some 2 billion claim to be Christians, leaving 4 billion totally outside of Christ. Many of these are still unreached, meaning that even if they wanted to hear the gospel there is not yet a viable, indigenous, evangelizing church movement within the group. In spite of the worldwide missionary movement, there are still multitudes of unreached ethnic groups with no churches or even Christians. Of the 2 billion who are called Christian (whether Protestant, Catholic or Orthodox) millions have not trusted Christ personally. Most nominal Christians know Christ died on a cross, but don't understand that salvation is through repentance and faith in Christ alone. This is the prevalent situation in much of Latin America, Europe and the Philippines (Asia's only so-called Christian nation.)

According to *Operation World*, some 4,000 socio-ethno-linguistic groups remain unreached. There are an estimated 1.5 billion people who have never heard the gospel. The number of people born in the non-Christian world grows by 129,000 a day, or 47 million a year according to research specialist David Barrett. The large unreached blocks of Muslim, Hindu and Buddhist peoples still represent a huge challenge.

Also the Bible isn't yet available to many language groups. Of the world's 7,148 languages, at least 2,000 still have a need for New Testament translation work and over 2,000 languages need to be surveyed to ascertain their need. Where the Scriptures have been translated, illiteracy prevents many from reading, and scarcity of Bibles often helps to make it an unknown book. Even in Western countries with churches on virtually every street corner, millions of secularists or humanists profess no religion at all.

In light of these facts, what kind of eternal significance do your current vocational plans hold?

_____

_____

Much attention in mission circles today is on the great cities of our world. According to David Barrett, urbanization is a major trend and not likely to change. Today half of the world's population live in cities. By 2000 there were 20 cities of over 10 million, 60 over 4 million and 402 over 1 million. Most of these cities are in the non-Western world and are non-Christian. The great surge of missions outreach in the late 20th century largely passed by the burgeoning urban population of the non-Western world. Christianity is being marginalized in many, if not most, of the world's largest cities. This will be one of the biggest challenges for missions in the 21st century when, by its close, 90 percent will be living in urban areas.

How will traditional missions have to change to keep up with the demands these realities imply? Think in terms of housing costs, safety, single women going out alone, etc.

_____

As Christians, we're fairly aware of the prayer concerns for our own cities, such as the plight of inner-city children, broken homes, drugs and crime. The cities described above are much larger than most of ours, and so are their problems. Would you be able to locate them on a world map? If not, take an hour some free evening to acquaint yourself a bit more thoroughly with a world map. A basic idea of geography is needed for you to be an informed world Christian.

ASIA'S CHALLENGE TO MISSIONS

A closer look at one part of the world, Asia, will reveal huge unmet needs for Christian missions. Asia is the world's most unreached continent. It holds over half the world's population, yet less than five percent are even nominally Christian! Christianity has more adherents than any other religion in five out of six of the world's continents. However, in the sixth and most populous continent (Asia), Christianity ranks sixth. There is still an enormous task in Asia! According to the *World Christian Encyclopedia* (Barrett, Kurian & Johnson 2001), 128 million East Asians were evangelicals in 2000, compared with 108 million in 1990—an increase of 19 percent. Sounds good! However, if we look at evangelicals as a proportion of the population, we find they are only 6.42 percent of the population, just 0.37 percent more than in 1990. The number of evangelicals in East Asia is just barely keeping up with the population growth.

Assignments: To my knowledge, the single most helpful resource tool for discovering what is happening in the world and the state of each nation in regards to the church, unmet needs and special opportunities is *Operation World* by Patrick Johnstone. This book will take you literally around the world in understanding the development of missions. It's designed to help you pray on a periodic or daily basis for each country. I recommend you get a copy of this incredible resource and commit yourself to reading it through in the next year with the suggested reading calendar.

Select one missionary your local church supports and find out as much as possible about his or her ministry and country of service. If little is available on file, write the person personally for further information. Ascertain the needs and opportunities where they serve for further missionary work.

WANTED: MISSIONARIES FOR STRATEGIC OPPORTUNITIES

We've just uncovered the tip of the iceberg. Huge needs exist and so do opportunities for ministry. Requests for the right kind of missionaries flow from mission agencies and from many developing or emerging churches needing teachers and trainers to help equip believers to reach their own people. Yes, in terms of need, missionaries are more in demand than ever.

In spite of political problems, there are more open doors than ever before in church history. Obviously some countries are closed to traditional missions or Western missionaries. These countries still represent a minority of the world's nations and certainly don't substantiate the popular myth that most countries are closed to the gospel. We have witnessed radical changes in Soviet bloc countries resulting in the opening of doors that were once closed.

In addition, even these so-called closed countries are not totally closed to Christians who may come in as foreign experts in professional roles. The whole area of tentmaking (more on that later)—that is, Christians taking secular employment or functioning as students while serving as witnesses and disciplers—is exploding with potential. Rather than using the term *restricted-access countries* in terms of traditional missionaries, we should be using the phrase *creative-access countries* to better describe the realities and opportunities for those who will see them. Already hundreds have gone out as Christian professionals to join other vocational missionaries in reaching the nations. But with only 85,000 Protestant foreign missionaries, many of whom are in church-nurture ministries, thousands more are needed to penetrate the unreached in the frontiers of our world.

According to Patrick Johnstone, of the 11,000 unreached people groups of the world, about 1,000 have no resident missionary work and insignificant numbers of believers. A further 2,000 people groups remain largely unreached, requiring pioneer mission-ary input. Even though we have more information than ever, there is no substitute for vision and commitment. Knowing facts and acting upon them are two different things. I pray as you continue to explore what needs and opportunities exist, you'll be sensitive to the Lord of the Harvest and like Isaiah be ready to say, "Here am I. Send me!" (Isa. 6:8)

Assignment: Brainstorm for five minutes on how your gifts and skills may be used to meet some of these needs.

MISSION TRENDS AND ISSUES

In completing this chapter, let's briefly survey the major trends and issues that confront missions today.

Some concerns relate to the setting of missions and others are linked to the nature of the work itself. All are highly relevant areas of which you should be aware.

1. **Strategy in missions.** In recent years, a great deal of attention has been paid to the question of how we should go about the task of evangelization. Included is the issue of whom we should seek to reach and the related priorities for allocation of personnel and resources. Dr. Ralph Winter of the U.S. Center for World Mission has been in the forefront of the frontier or hidden-peoples movement since he introduced the concept at the Lausanne Conference on World Evangelization in 1974.

   Winter stresses the highest priority for missions today is cross-cultural evangelism to the truly unreached people groups of the world. He adds that serving existing churches has value, but the emphasis of new personnel and resources, along with strategy formulation should be to penetrate those groups without an internal Christian movement that is able to adequately evangelize its own people. The rationale behind this emphasis is that with the establishment of a viable, indigenous, evangelizing (reproducing) church, the group (walled off from others by barriers of cultural understanding and language) has the potential to hear and respond to the gospel in a contextually positive way. Until that breakthrough occurs, there can be no culturally relevant witness. This challenge to reach the some 4,000 unreached people groups of the world has stirred a fair amount of debate and interest, but is a dominant concept in evangelical circles today.

2. **Church-growth theory.** Dr. Donald McGavran has become a household name in missions since the introduction of his first book on church growth in the 1950s. Since then he has led a movement to stimulate both foreign and domestic churches to consider seriously the biblical, sociological, political and other factors that both aid or hinder church growth in a given place. Terms such as the "homogeneous-unit principle" have been coined by McGavran to underscore the realization that people like to become Christians and grow as Christians without having to cross cultural barriers. He stresses that God works through family and social structures, a truth which can be well documented from patterns in the New Testament.

A more recent emphasis in missions' strategy and church growth centers on the "Church-planting Movements" theory. A CPM is a "rapid and multiplicative increase of indigenous churches planting churches within a given people group or population segment." The focus is on developing a movement, not just individual churches, and therefore focusing on reproducibility rather than short-term goals. The missionary's role is that of a catalyst, mentor, trainer, who is empowering nationals, rather than as a planter, pastor and teacher who is leading nationals. At any rate, it behooves missionaries to align their strategies and methods with God's wisdom and sound principles if they would see the kind of church growth he intends.

3. **Urban missions.** While relating to strategy, urban ministries have become a major trend in recent years. Numerous conferences, seminars and workshops have been held in order to raise awareness of the need of the cities and hammer out workable strategies. Many mission agencies are developing urban teams and committing personnel and resources as never before. Of course, work in the inner cities requires special skills and people and represents one of the greatest challenges to the church today.

4. **Outreach to ethnic minorities and internationals.** Truly the mission field has come to most of our traditional sending countries. In the United States, for instance, there are some 500,000 international students who present a unique opportunity for evangelism. A number of U.S.-based mission agencies recognize that newcomers and immigrants to the States

from the traditionally foreign fields are strategic, and have placed ministry teams to reach them here.

It's staggering to realize that America receives over 1 million newcomers each year. This, along with the population growth of current ethnic minority groups, is rapidly changing the demographic mix of the U.S. At present almost 50 cities in the States have an ethnic majority. For example, Los Angeles is now 72 percent non-anglo-American. In fact, Los Angeles has the second largest Spanish population in the world, next only to Mexico City. In the Houston, Texas, school system 80 percent of the students are of African, Asian or Hispanic descent. New York City is the second largest Puerto Rican city. And the list could go on.

The same picture could be painted in Canada, Western Europe and elsewhere. In Germany, for instance, large numbers of Turks and other people from Arab countries have immigrated for work purposes and therefore represent a special opportunity for reaching them there, since it is highly difficult in their homelands. Missions have had to rethink what is "field" and what is "home." The two have significantly merged in recent years and thus our strategies need to keep pace with this critical development.

How do you react to new ethnic groups entering your community?

_____

_____

_____

_____

What ethnic groups are located in your community? Are there viable, indigenous, evangelizing churches among them? What groups in your community are most favorably positioned to reach out to them?

_____

_____

_____

List some ways you could use this opportunity for evangelism.

_____

_____

_____

5. **Evangelism and social action.** For years there has been much ferment and debate in Christian circles on the issue of evangelism and social action. Some contend that evangelism is the primary concern of the church and so either downgrade or neglect social concern. Others have argued that social action is the chief task of the church today and thus tend to make it a substitute for evangelism. In their extremes, these polarities have been seen in the

expressions of the conciliar movement of which the World Council of Churches would be a part, and in the evangelical movement on the other side. Behind this debate are some critical theological issues and assumptions.

However, within evangelical circles there's been a growing consensus that evangelism and social concern aren't unrelated, that both, in fact, form the legitimate Christian response to the world. The Lausanne Covenant of 1974 clarified these two issues and their interplay in the following statement: "In the church's mission of sacrificial service, evangelism is primary." At the same time, the covenant went on to affirm that social responsibility may follow evangelism as its consequence, precede it as its bridge or accompany it as its social responsibility. In the end, evangelism is still seen as the unique and ultimate need for all mankind.

6. **The gospel and culture.** How does the gospel relate to culture and in what ways may the gospel be culturally adapted in communicating effectively? Contextualization is currently in the forefront of missiological thinking. Numerous articles, books and even conferences have dealt at length with the related issues. This debate has been particularly focused in recent years on evangelistic approaches to Muslim cultures where there is considerable

resistance to the Christian message. Within the missions community, however, there is still a spectrum of understanding about what is an appropriate (biblically allowable) approach and what may seem culturally necessary and helpful in reaching a Muslim group.

The question is in the relationship between the structure and expression of Christianity in a given cultural setting. Biblical contextualization seeks to faithfully convey the biblical message in terms and ways that are relevant to the context of the receptor culture.

7. **The Holy Spirit and evangelism.** Emerging afresh in recent years is a re-emphasis on the role of the Holy Spirit in church growth and evangelism. Related to this is an awareness of spiritual warfare, and the need for power encounters as part of the evangelistic effort. Prayer walks, spiritual mapping and terms like "territorial spirits" have been introduced but are still somewhat controversial.

8. **The local church and missions.** In recent years a new paradigm for sending churches has emerged. More local churches are now sensing their responsibilities to direct their missionary efforts and are operating either independent of traditional mission agencies or demanding a closer working partner-

ship and accountability with mission agencies. Serious questions are being asked about who should go, how funds should be spent and who directs the missionary. There has been a shift in many churches from the traditional style of supporting (no questions asked) to a sending posture (where the church is more proactive in defining and directing the task) and a synergistic pattern of working in partnership with agencies or national entities in pursuing their vision and goals. Also there has been a major shift in many churches from the traditional pattern of sending missionaries long term to engagement of the church with projects which tend to be of a shorter duration.

9. **Short-term missions.** There is no doubt about it— short-term missions are here to stay! The numbers of people going out from one week to two years has dramatically increased. The whole meaning of the word "missionary" has been redefined. No longer is the mission field seen as the province of a few elite career missionaries. Increasingly, "ordinary" lay people are finding that they can also contribute to the missions enterprise with their time and talents. Proponents of short-term missionary service assert that short-termers will enlarge the pool of long-term, career missionaries, and in addition, increase the pool of goodwill towards missions while pray-

ing, giving and advocating missions when back home. However, short-term missions can also have a negative side. As Stan Guthrie states, "Short-term work, whether two weeks or two years, can indeed be effective and pleasing to God. Yes, it can cost a lot of money, disrupt nationals and missionaries, encourage short-term thinking, and inoculate some against career missions involvement. But done well, it can open participants' eyes to the sometimes gritty realities of the world, make them aware of their own ethno-centrism and the gifts and courage of non-Western believers, and spark a lifelong commitment to missions. In the best cases, some real kingdom work gets done, too."

10. **Tentmaking missions.** As mentioned before, with the ever-changing geo-political scene, missions must adapt to the visa limitations of restricted-access countries as well as seek to multiply the effectiveness of many professional or business-related Christians living abroad. Increasingly, tentmaking will be seen as a major strategy for evangelism and efforts will be made to recruit, train and send them along with traditional vocational missionaries.

11. **Supporting nationals.** Seeking the help of "nationals" is a growing trend in our world and this is true not only for international business but with respect

to the local church in thinking about missions as well. Some churches look at both the high costs of supporting a traditional missionary from home and the question of ministry effectiveness in a foreign language and culture, and conclude that it makes sense to support nationals instead. Thus we have the phenomena today of "missions by checkbook"! However, there needs to be balance and careful accountability of resources in order to avoid disasters. The church that sends only money may in time lose its vision and concern for missions altogether. Likewise, inordinate dependence on outside funding can create serious problems for national workers and the church itself. What is needed is a a commitment by the local sending church to genuine partnerships and wise stewardship of resources. There is ample room for both sending missionaries and partnering appropriately with national colleagues in the missions enterprise.

SUMMARY

There is no doubt that the world of missions is in rapid change today. In looking ahead to preparation for service, it's very important for you to seek to keep abreast of the major developments. As a way of helping you stay informed, I would suggest that you subscribe to the *Evangelical Missions Quarterly* and *Pulse*, which are published by the Evangelical Missions Information

Service in Wheaton, Illinois. Another helpful resource is *Mission Frontiers*, put out monthly by the U.S. Center for World Mission in Pasadena, California.

Think through the missions program at your church. How does it keep the congregation informed of major developments and needs in missions? What more could be done? How can you help?

_____

_____

_____

_____

For further study, I recommend the following:

Guthrie, Stan. *Missions in the Third Millennium: 21 Key Trends for the 21st Century*, Paternoster Press, 2000.

5

understanding the local church, missions and you

Several years ago I interviewed a young college graduate who was very interested in missionary work in Japan. He excitedly told me all about how the Lord had called him and placed a deep desire on his heart to go. After listening, I asked if he had shared his "call" to service with his church leaders yet. His reply was a rather puzzled, "What have they got to do with it?"

Unfortunately many potential missionary candidates fail to see the relevancy of the local church to their own particular call to go, other than a hope that the church will provide support once they've gone. What is worse is the fact that all too often local churches aren't really aware of their role in the whole selecting, training, sending and supporting process for potential missionaries coming out of their local congregations.

After many years of experience, I'm convinced that

missionaries shouldn't just go, but be *sent*. Would you agree with this statement? If so, what are the implications for you at this stage in your developing interest? And what should you do if your church doesn't share your vision or lacks vision entirely?

THE BARNABAS MODEL

Let's take a look at Barnabas, missionary colleague to the Apostle Paul. He is a helpful role model for understanding the important link between the local church and its missionaries. We're first introduced to Barnabas in Acts 4:36-37. Who was Barnabas?

_____

What character qualities are displayed in his life?

_____

Later we find Barnabas involved in the church at Antioch in Acts 11:22-24. Why was he sent to Antioch?

_____

_____

From Acts 11:25-30, what other qualities or abilities do you see in Barnabas' life?

_____

_____

The account of Paul and Barnabas being sent from

Antioch on the first missionary journey holds some important factors you need to grasp to understand the role of the local church in your life as a potential missionary. Acts 13:1-4 gives a description of the "call" and "sending" of Barnabas and Paul. First of all, how were these two men already involved in the church at Antioch?

_____

_____

_____

What was the Holy Spirit's command to the church?

_____

_____

Why do you think the Holy Spirit spoke to the church on this occasion and not directly to Paul and Barnabas?

_____

_____

Look carefully at verses 3 and 4. Who really sent these first missionaries in each verse? How do you synthesize these two statements?

_____

_____

A careful scrutiny of the above passage reveals several critical elements with application for us today. First, the local church had a part in the guidance and sending of its missionaries. In reality the Apostle Paul had already received a personal call to be a missionary to the Gentiles at the moment of his conversion (Acts 9:15). God then used the local church to confirm that personal call and direct the timing of his going. Secondly, the local church had a part in both the release of Paul and Barnabas as well as their commissioning (Acts 13:3). This apparently established a relationship of accountability which is demonstrated in Acts 14:26. When the two missionaries returned to Antioch at the close of the first journey, they reported to the church from which they "...had been committed to the grace of God for the work they had now completed."

How do you see this pattern demonstrated in the relationship between your church and missionaries today?

_____

_____

THE LOCAL CHURCH CO-SENDS

Obviously the local church has a vital relationship with a potential missionary. But we need to clarify one other aspect of this partnership, and that is where the final authority for sending is. Is it the local church? Or the mission agency? A look back at Acts 13:3-4 will hopefully clarify this question. You need to know this in order to keep the lines of accountability straight.

The specific command to the Antioch church was that Paul and Barnabas be "released." In response we read that after a special time of prayer and fasting, they "sent them off." However, in 13:4 the Holy Spirit is described as the one who "sent them on their way." At first you may feel confused as to who really sent these missionaries, the church or the Holy Spirit. This confusion can be cleared by understanding the Greek words in Acts 13:3-4 translated as sent. In the first instance the word *apoluo* is used, meaning to dismiss, release or send off. In conjunction with the Holy Spirit in Acts 13:4, a different Greek word is used, *ekpempo*, which as a compound verb is almost synonymous with *apostello*, meaning to send with authority on an authorized mission.

Who, then, sends the missionary? Paul Beals explains:

> Ultimately, God the Holy Spirit is the sending agent in the church's mission. This is the vertical aspect of sending. The church at Antioch through their spiritual leaders let Barnabas and Saul go their way at the Spirit's prompting. This is the horizontal aspect. Our churches today need to recapture the vitality of this divine-human plan for sending missionaries.[1]

This means that the ultimate authority for sending is Christ (Matt. 28:19), but the local or home church becomes the mediating authority through which the call may be confirmed to you. This is the ideal relationship between the local church and the potential missionary.

I'm aware that this concept isn't always followed. If a church is disobedient to the Great Commission or insensitive to mission needs, God may bypass the ideal sending process in order to call out laborers into the harvest. Many historical illustrations could be mentioned. Nevertheless, the so-called missionary call is best recognized and nurtured in a congregation. Your home church is very important to you as a potential missionary.

THE LOCAL CHURCH SELECTS

In recent centuries, the normal pattern for missionary recruitment has been the volunteer system. Coupled with this is the idea of a personal, subjective missionary call. The result seems to leave many young people to make major decisions for missionary service without reference to their local church. What are the implications of this approach? If you decide to become a missionary without input from your pastor or missions committee, what might be complications later on?

_____

_____

Let's check it out with Scripture and see if this is the pattern used there. In Acts, people are chosen for leadership roles. Their acceptability is not based on their availability or volunteering. For example, what about Barnabas whom we looked at earlier? How was he chosen to go first to Antioch and then later with Paul on the first missionary journey (Acts 11, 13)?

_____

_____

_____

On what basis was Silas selected as Paul's companion missionary, and Mark rejected (Acts 15:22, 30-32, 37-40)?

_____

_____

_____

And finally, as an example, how about Timothy? Did he volunteer or was he selected (Acts 16:1-3)?

_____

_____

Michael Griffiths, in *Get Your Church Involved in Missions*, summarizes the pattern in Acts this way:

> Whereas we seem to have emphasized exclusively the individual's subjective sense of a personal call of God, and often reinforced this by emotional appeals for individuals to volunteer, the New Testament by contrast stresses either the corporate initiative of congregations, or the informed

initiative of missionaries in selecting suitable people.

This all boils down to the need to relate your major decisions about missions to your local church. Why? So you will get the right kind of counsel and input about your basic suitability and areas of giftedness. Secondly, you can then receive the kind of preparation and training to best equip you for your future ministry in missions. Finally, your church needs to take ownership of decisions and stand behind you in financial support and many other practical ways. This doesn't imply you have no freedom of choice or should seek permission for every career decision. But God normally uses the Body of Christ to lead us, and to bypass them is to cut us off from a valuable source of wisdom and practical help.

Griffiths comments further about the shortcomings of the volunteer system as an encouragement to see the bigger picture. What are the weaknesses of the volunteer system?

1. A coach does not build a football team by volunteers. He selects the best players available. There is even less wisdom in selecting ambassadors by calling for volunteers at random. Why be less selective in seeking ambassadors for the King of kings?

2. If churches send only those who have responded to emotional appeals at the end of emotional meetings, only the more emotional people will respond. Some

people are uncomfortable in those settings and eliminate themselves from service by default. A more rational basis for candidate selection should accompany the ways God moves people to decisions.

3. Considerable pressure is placed upon mission agencies in candidate selection if the church doesn't do its job first. Many young people invest considerable time in preparation and training, only to be told later by a mission agency that they are unqualified for service. The disillusionment to the individual, not to mention the embarrassment to the local church, can be extremely painful. The individual concerned, as well as the congregation, deserves honest and fair assessment from their church leaders.

4. The volunteer system has failed to produce either the numbers or the quality of candidates needed to meet the pressing needs in the world today. Nearly all mission societies are facing serious personnel shortages just to maintain their current level of outreach. Stronger, more effective action is required to accomplish today's mission than simply waiting for people to offer to serve.

5. A further deficiency in the volunteer system can be seen in the imbalance in the types of candidates applying to agencies. Specialists in limited areas may offer to serve, but the number of evangelist/church planters—needed to carry out basic missionary activity—is woefully inadequate. If

churches take a more active role, then greater numbers of the right kind of needed workers will be forthcoming.[2]

Although more will be said about agencies in Chapter Ten, let me underscore the critical need to keep both the local church and the mission agency in perspective as you consider options for service and the application process. As we've established, the sending authority for missions is Christ and the local church is the mediating authority (with sensitivity to the Holy Spirit and the personal sense of call of the missionary candidate).

Because most local churches aren't in a position to operate their own mission work directly, they work through agencies. As a result, the agency can be seen as the implementing authority in the chain. At the same time, some churches feel that they are equipped and have the resources to send directly without partnering with a mission agency. This is certainly a legitimate pattern. However, unless the sending church has the personnel and resources to adequately direct the ministry, assist with the necessary logistics and provide the appropriate pastoral care, it might be best to partner with an agency. Agencies have built up considerable experience through the years, and because they have on-site resources to help the new missionaries especially in the early days of adjustment, language study and integration into the work, not to mention children's education, they can be a great asset in insuring a successful ministry. How, then, should the church relate to the agencies? Is the church obligated to accept any mission agency in which you as a potential candidate are interested?

Mission boards are becoming more and more aware of the need to work in close cooperation with local churches regarding potential candidates. OMF International, of which I am a part, is working to establish specific partnerships with cooperating churches. Our aim is to find churches compatible with our policies, ethos and ministry objectives so that we can be channels they can use to send some of their suitable candidates to Asia (where our primary work is focused). Once they understand our agency, partnership churches seek to select, train and send personnel through us. We, in turn, try to serve those churches with information, resource materials, personnel and close accountability to help them fulfill their missions educational, mobilization and supervision tasks. This way local churches and agencies can do a better job in matching the right people with the right needs to perform effective ministries.

There are two streams of thought as to how the church should engage in mission and relate to agencies. David Dougherty of OMF International has labeled these as *missions as process*, and *missions as project*. They are basically two ways a church can be involved in missionary activity. Missions as process is the more traditional approach and focuses on sending and supporting workers for the long haul. Missions as project would look more at involvement through short-term missionaries and specific projects that are seen to be strategic. These two paradigms can be contrasted as follows.

Missions as process	Missions as project
Fulfilling Great Commission	Reaching unreached
Focused on activities	Focused on achievement
Defined broadly	Accomplishing tasks
Long-term, open-ended	Short-term, projects
Recruits "called" people	Uses volunteers
Values professional training and experience	Preparation is usually church-based
Invest in infrastructure	Largely ignore structures
Focus on existing work	Focus on 10/40, unreached
Agency-driven	Church-driven

In reality, both approaches are necessary and legitimate and we should avoid an either-or situation. Conservative missiology needs to combine with progressive methodology. Project within process is helpful as an approach, and long-term process may need to develop from short-term project.

THE LOCAL CHURCH SUPPORTS

While visiting a major missions-minded church recently, I heard one of the pastors make an all too familiar comment: "Missionaries and agencies simply look at us like a bank auto-teller machine!" What a sad commentary! When the local church is taken out of the selection, training and vocational consultation loop, then it is understandable for candidates or agencies to see churches as a bank to fund their ministries. But what is the role of the local church in financing missions?

When a church truly sends a missionary they back their commitment with financial support. Churches and pastors don't appreciate being the last to hear someone from their congregation is going to the mission field. When the church is brought into the process from the beginning, they can be a part of the entire process. Then there is a much better opportunity for them to be substantially involved in financial support than when their input is bypassed. When churches are adequately consulted and involved, their sense of ownership and full participation is more likely.

YOUR ROLE AND OPPORTUNITY

Now that we've established the importance of the local church in the missions sending process, let's think through some practical ways in which you can strengthen ties with your church and involve them in your planning and preparation right from the beginning.

1. Inform your pastor and other significant persons (mission committee personnel or even Sunday school teachers) of your interest and sense of guidance. Opening lines of communication lets them know you're available and willing for their help and input. Perhaps it would be best to phrase your interest initially as "I'm seriously considering missions, but what do you think?" This is much preferable to a firm and non-negotiable, "God has called me and I'm going!" A submissive attitude to the wisdom of godly leaders in your church will stand you in good stead in the future. In fact, the Bible has a fair amount to say about corporate guidance. Check out these references and see what advice they offer.

Proverbs 11:14

_____

_____

_____

Proverbs 15:22

_____

_____

_____

Proverbs 16:1-3

_____

_____

Proverbs 20:18

_____

_____

Colossians 3:15-17

_____

_____

Hebrews 13:17

_____

_____

2. Look for special classes or interest groups in your church geared toward missions and ministry. A growing number of churches are developing programs to help people become aware of world missions and start preparation for cross-cultural service. Find out what's going on in your church and see what's available. If there is a missions committee already, a committee member will likely be able to direct you into the right program.

3. Avoid commitments to mission agencies before your church has interacted with you and them. As

an agency, we contact the applicant's home church at the preliminary level, to obtain an assessment of the potential candidate before going any further. It is fine to talk with agencies and get information, but it is counter-productive to make major commitments to placement and training without your church's involvement.

Some of you face a dilemma at this point. Your church isn't that sympathetic to missions and may not know how to advise and help you. It is important that you help them. You may suggest that your pastor or others read the following resource materials:

Who, Me? A Missionary? by Daniel W. Bacon, OMF Books, 1985.

A People for His Name by Paul A. Beals, Baker Book House, 1988.

Get Your Church Involved in Mission by Michael Griffiths, OMF Books, 1987.

Encourage a mission representative to discuss with your church helpful ways to direct and prepare a missionary candidate. Special agencies such as the Association of Church Missions Committees (ACMC) <http://community.gospelcom.net> would be delighted to serve as resources to your church .

1 Paul A. Beals, *A People for His Name*, Baker, 1988, p.62.
2 Michael Griffiths, *Get Your Church Involved in Mission*, OMF Books, 1972, p.13.

6

developing a personal strategy for missions involvement

The old cliché that says the longest journey begins with the first step has a certain element of truth for us. Over the years as I've watched many young people face all the implications of serious missions involvement, I've seen several different reactions. Some panic at the thought of years of training and preparation and feel it's a mountain too high to climb. Others are looking for the next plane out of the country and can't be easily convinced that preparation is necessary. Another group of young people, overwhelmed at all of the options and programs, are semi-paralyzed, not knowing where to begin.

The purpose of this chapter is to help you start your journey on the right foot and hopefully not get lost or discouraged en route. The choices you need to make aren't quite as complicated as you think. There are also quite a few competent guides and resources to help you on your way.

Keep in mind that any serious commitment to serve Christ as a missionary will be contested by the enemy. Don't be surprised or intimidated when obstacles or confusion arrives. Arthur Mathews offered budding missionaries this pastoral rendition of Shakespeare: "There's many a slip between the call and the ship." Nonetheless, God promises to guide and provide for us. He is equal to the task and will continue to enable us for whatever task he calls us to do.

STEPS IN THE CAREER PATH

I have always found it helpful in starting a journey to see the whole trip on a map before working out specific details. Let's map out an overview of what you will face on the missions career path. Some of what follows will also be helpful and applicable to those of you who only have a short-term involvement in mind at this stage.

Missionary Life Cycle: Developmental Tasks. There is certain predictability to the life and work of a cross-cultural missionary. Knowing something of what's ahead should enable you to face the preparation with more realistic expectations. You will then see missionary life as a career with certain phases or tasks.

1. **The guidance task.** Already you are dealing with

the questions of who, how, where and when if God is leading you into missions. Basic questions about your suitability and with whom and where you should work need to be addressed.

2. **The education task.** You will likely have to face the possibility of further education in biblical, missiological and professional studies. No one becomes a brain surgeon without some training, and the same expectations are likely for you in career missions.

3. **The training task.** Part of your preparation will be in practical areas such as working in a local church or with para-church ministries. Cross-cultural experience may also be advised and may include a short-term stint.

4. **The application and sending task.** Assuming you plan to work with an established missions agency, you must select the appropriate one. Choosing the agency and completing the application process should be done in conjunction with your home church. Then comes the probability of the deputation phase (raising sufficient support) and, finally, being commissioned and sent for service.

5. **The entry task.** Once on your field, you'll focus on adapting to a new culture and language. While difficult, fluency in your target language and successful cultural adaptation are vital if you are to be effective.

6. **The organizational integration task.** We often joke

about the idealism of young engaged couples looking towards a "perfect marriage" through starry eyes. The gap between expectations and reality is often considerable and may come as quite a shock. So is the adjustment to the mission agency or ministry situation on the field. Without effective organizational integration, a missionary may not be able to function.

7. **The role integration task.** Another important phase in a missionary career is adapting to the many roles of the work. These include relations with missionary colleagues, nationals, family, mission board and sending churches.

8. **Family education task.** Should God give you a life partner and children, an obvious and crucial task is working through the educational needs of each child. This area represents one of the biggest challenges to any missionary and needs special wisdom and attention. The educational alternatives are considerable and appropriate solutions need to be provided.

9. **The transition task.** Missionaries find themselves frequently on the move. Changes between field and home for furloughs add special pressures and require the ability to adapt and handle transition.

10. **The professional task.** As time goes by, most missionaries realize the need for further professional training and personal enrichment. Advanced

degrees may be required. Furloughs can be a time for study or specialized training. A willingness to upgrade and grow help significantly in developing a healthy missions career.

11. **Adult family care task.** This may seem a long way off but the possibility of caring responsibly for aging parents or other dependents is something each of us must face. Many missionaries find themselves having to leave the field temporarily to care for family members. The implications of this need to be considered even at the beginning of your missionary career.

12. **Retirement-reintegration task.** Assuming missions becomes a life commitment, positive planning for the retirement phase merits consideration. When returning from the field, fruitful ministry need not cease. It's helpful to think ahead about the redeployment and ongoing use of your experience along with the practical logistics of retirement.

ASSESSING WHERE YOU ARE

Now that we've had a quick overview of the various possible phases of a missions career, it's time to stop and see where you are in your journey. Here is a checklist of basic questions to help you assess your present situation and suggestions for planning the next steps. See where your strengths or areas of need are located.

Personal Activities

	Yes	No
I'm spending time daily in Bible study and prayer.	❏	❏
I'm seeking to obey Scriptures in daily living.	❏	❏
I'm actively witnessing as opportunities arise.	❏	❏
I'm seeking to use my spiritual gifts in service.	❏	❏
I'm open to go wherever God should lead.	❏	❏

Missions Awareness

	Yes	No
I'm reading a mission-agency periodical regularly.	❏	❏
I'm praying regularly for a missionary.	❏	❏
I'm reading a missionary biography or missions book.	❏	❏
I'm watching world news from a missions perspective.	❏	❏
I'm learning about the missions program at my church.	❏	❏
I'm writing to a missionary for information and prayer.	❏	❏
I'm attending mission conferences where possible.	❏	❏
I'm relating to international students or immigrants.	❏	❏

Church Relations

I'm involved in my local church in
attendance and service. ❏ ❏

I've spoken with the pastor or missions
committee about my missions interest. ❏ ❏

I've identified the mission agencies my
church supports. ❏ ❏

I've written to several mission boards for
information. ❏ ❏

Training and Experience

I've discovered what are the basic
educational requirements of at least three
mission agencies. ❏ ❏

I've been on or am planning a summer
missions project. ❏ ❏

I've discussed with the missions committee
practical ways to prepare for missionary
service. ❏ ❏

Well, how are you doing? The point isn't to intimidate
you with a huge to-do list, but to help you be realistic
about where you are in the process. Find any serious
gaps in the above areas? Work with your church (if you
possibly can) to develop a practical plan for moving
ahead. It's an exciting process in which God will lead
you as you depend upon him for guidance and wisdom.

Before moving on, there are several other critical

areas to be carefully evaluated. In effect, these areas determine in part one's suitability or even availability for missionary service. Answer the following questions as honestly and objectively as possible.

1. **Family Circumstances.** The mission field puts considerable stress on any family and therefore each member has to be ready for it. Wives serve not only as mothers and homemakers, but are also a vital part of the work. Family size is also important. Coping in language school with three or four pre-school children to look after may be too much for you. Overall support costs are based on family size, and should be realistically kept in mind. Temporary separation from children for schooling may be a part of missionary life, or the realities of home schooling without the support group you may have back at home. All these facts need honest consideration to see if each member is prepared and able to meet the challenge and demands.

   Unfortunately, some husbands have pushed their wives onto the mission field without giving adequate attention to her own sense of call or commitment to the task. Frequently, the pressure becomes unbearable and a premature return home results.

   More and more older families with school-age children are going to the field for the first time.

While parents may come with a degree of maturity and experience, children might come in for a jolt. Careful attention must be given to the adjustments they must face.

Another important area which has to be addressed frankly is divorce. This is a sensitive and complex issue involving not only the individual but also the sending church, mission agency and receiving or national church. The cultural perspective in the host country is an important factor. Thus some mission boards have policies barring candidates with divorce in their background, while others accept them, assuming all other qualifications are satisfactory. It would be helpful to seek counsel both with your home church and any prospective mission agencies before you make long-term plans.

Checklist
Is there anything in my family circumstances that would prevent me from going overseas?
❏ My spouse isn't willing/isn't well enough/doesn't have suitable gifts or training.
❏ We have more than two children.
❏ We have a child with special needs.
❏ Divorce is in our background.
❏ Other

Have I taken into consideration the needs of my spouse

or children in the decision making process?

❑ Yes

❑ No

I plan, however, to _____

_____

If currently single, am I seeking a life partner who is truly compatible with my missionary goals?

❑ Yes

❑ No

I need to _____

_____

Are my parents' attitudes or needs a barrier to my going overseas?

❑ Yes

❑ No

A solution might be _____

_____

2. **Physical and mental health.** Good personal or family health is needed in cross-cultural ministry. Living in a foreign culture with climatic differences puts considerable stress on the physical and emotional stamina of the missionary. Physical weakness tends to be accentuated on the field. Therefore, you'll need to be able to cope under stress and handle the demands of a much simpler lifestyle.

A sad fact of 21st century life is that a large sector of Christian young people come out of broken homes or the drug culture. Emotional scars are inevitable. Many of us carry emotional baggage from dysfunctional homes or relationships. While the grace of God is always operative in the believer, the consequences of one's background and vulnerability to the pressures of cross-cultural living need to be realistically faced. A history of depression or other emotional problems can't be taken lightly. An honest assessment of emotional weaknesses or areas of vulnerability is a wise precaution and helpful factor in discerning God's place for you. While weakness is common to us all, we need counsel to make sure that we are realistic about the mission field and that there are adequate resources there to cope. If not, then redirection might be in order.

Physical disabilities aren't quite the automatic bar to missionary work they used to be, but neither can they be ignored. Some missionary roles may be filled by those with handicaps or certain health limitations; but generally speaking, it is unwise to consider missions if one has a history of health problems or chronic weakness. It may seem brave and spiritual to offer for service in spite of physical weaknesses, but might not be wise. Experience proves the hard realities of burdens and liabilities sometimes placed on fellow workers and administration (not to mention the expense factor) when emotional and physical limitations in candidates are not seen as limitations.

Checklist

Do I have any physical limitations?

❏ Yes

❏ No

Yes, but I could manage if _____

_____

Am I able now to cope with the normal stress and demands of life and ministry?

❏ Yes

❏ No

❏ Usually

Are there aspects of my past that need to be dealt with perhaps by counseling?

❏ Yes

❏ No

❏ Counseling is in my plans

3. **Prior commitments.** Unfortunately, finishing school without any kind of financial debt is rare these days for many young people. By the time university or seminary preparation is completed, many face the challenge of considerable debt. Ideally churches

and agencies want to see missionaries going to the field without any encumbrances recognizing the stress or complications that could bring. That might mean a period of employment to erase the debt. However, agencies vary in their policies about going to the field with outstanding loans or other financial responsibilities such as the care of parents. It is wise to discuss this area with your church leadership as well as with agency personnel.

DETERMINING YOUR PRIORITY NEEDS

When the journey seems long and the preparation demands many, it's easy to try to rush things. A wise missionary once told me, "It's not going that counts, but what you do when you get there." Think through your priorities for preparation. Develop a practical sequence of implementing them. You need not do everything at once. I urge you to begin with the following.

1. **Establish lines of accountability.** As I've mentioned before, act in concert with the spiritual leaders of your church if at all possible. If you haven't done so already, make an appointment to talk with the missions committee or pastor. If you are away at school, you may want to write a letter.

   Share your vision or interest in missions and ask for specific guidelines or next steps. Set up an accountability system so that they routinely check your progress towards preparation and development goals. What are their recommendations?

2. **Clarify your priorities for growth and training.** Based on your level of training, experience and readiness, outline a series of next steps.

   To crystallize your planning further, set specific plans and dates to your ideas. These ideas are adapted from the MARC article, *You Can So Get There From Here.* If you don't know how and when some of these things can be implemented, talk matters over with your pastor or missions committee. A mission agency representative can likely be of help also.

   a. I will complete these educational needs by the dates listed:

   Need: _____

   Date: _____

   b. I will contact the following mission agencies:

   Agency: _____

   _____

   Date: _____

   c. I will research the following opportunities and needs:

   Needs: _____

   Date: _____

d. I will engage in the following cross-cultural experiences:
Experience: _____
Date: _____

e. I will finish the following advanced training experiences:
Training: _____
Date: _____

In summary, please keep in mind that your career path may vary from someone else's. Because the expectations of mission agencies vary considerably, it is helpful to know what is ahead and required as early as possible. At the same time, remember that God has the right to change "our plans." I think of the Apostle Paul in Acts 16, attempting to evangelize what is now North Central Turkey:

> Paul and his companions traveled throughout the region of Phyrgia and Galatia, having been kept by the Holy Spirit from preaching the word in the province of Asia. When they came to the border of Mysia, they tried to enter Bithynia, but the Spirit of Jesus would not allow them to. So they passed by Mysia and went down to Troas. During the night Paul had a vision of a man of Macedonia standing and begging him, "Come over and help us." (Acts 16:6-7)

So, while we should be open and flexible to God's "Plan B," it's also helpful to have specific goals and plans to move us along on the journey even if he changes them from time to time. Preparatory steps are seldom, if ever, wasted.

7

Deciding if you should stay or go

The missions conference was coming to a close. The final speaker faced his audience with keen anticipation, looking intensely for some kind of response to the challenge of his message. Now was the moment of decision. "Who tonight senses the call of God to missions? Who will step out in obedience and offer himself to the Lord of the harvest? The fields are ripe, but the laborers are few. If God is calling, don't hold back."

Sound familiar? Unfortunately at this particular missions conference a puzzled student turned to a friend and quipped, "I don't get it. If God is calling, why is he so hard to hear? How can I know for sure if God is really calling me and not my next-door neighbor?"

No question comes up as frequently or creates as much confusion in mission conferences or meetings than the whole matter of the "missionary call." This term has been debated, dissected and analyzed in recent years with both heat and light emerging from the process. Some have reduced the so-called "missionary call" to a neat formula. Others feel the term is unbiblical and harmful and so discourage its use. Meanwhile the average Christian is being challenged with the needs and opportunities of the many mission fields of our world and struggles to know what the call is all about and if he or she has one.

Let's see where you are in your current thinking. Please check in response to the following statements, which you feel are true or false:

T__ F__ Everyone should head for missions until God stops him.

T__ F__ Don't be a missionary if you can be happier doing something else.

T__ F__ According to the Great Commission, all believers are already called and thus you don't need further guidance.

T__ F__ Don't move towards missions until God gives you a call.

T__ F__ If you are needed somewhere and suitably gifted, that constitutes a call.

T__ F__ A missionary call is a special spiritual and emotional experience, and when you receive it, you'll know it for sure.

Confused yet? No wonder most of us are, with all of the

differing opinions. The concept of the missionary call comes to us today with a long tradition and even stronger emotions. It is difficult to distinguish between the factual and fictional aspects of it.

USE OF CALL IN SCRIPTURE

The word "call" is certainly not foreign to the Bible. The Greek word, *kaleo*, usually translated "call," occurs 148 times in the New Testament with an additional 70 times in related terms.

In the following passages, what is the primary use of the word call, and how is it applied?

Romans 8:28

_____

_____

Romans 9:24-26

_____

_____

1 Corinthians 1:2

_____

_____

Galatians 1:6

_____

_____

Ephesians 4:1

_____

_____

Many other similar verses could be mentioned as well.
As you can see from the above verses, the predominant
use of the term *call* is in reference to God's calling of
individuals to salvation and to a quality of life as a
Christian. We could describe this as God's *general call*.

At the same time, there are several other uses of the
term *call* found in Scripture. How are these applied?

Romans 1:1

_____

_____

1 Corinthians 1:1

_____

_____

Acts 13:2

_____

_____

Acts 16:9-10

_____

_____

_____

Obviously Paul saw himself as an apostle, called and appointed by the will of God (Eph. 3:7). He saw his ministry as part of God's calling in his life (Acts 13:2). It also seems the Bible uses the term in reference to service. That is, we are all called to salvation and a Christian walk worthy of that calling (Eph. 4:1). Beyond that, some are called to Christian service or ministry, as Paul and Barnabas in Acts 13:2. But what about the term *missionary call*? Do you feel there is a unique vocational or geographic call that is necessary for service?

_____

How would you describe or define it?

_____

_____

_____

It is important to note, however, that the only time geography is used in relation to a call in the New Testament is in Acts 16:10. Do you think it still legitimate for us to use a phrase such as, "I'm called to Japan?" Why or why not?

_____

_____

_____

Furthermore, there is no record of any individual in the Book of Acts being accepted or rejected on Paul's apostolic mission band because of a personal call. The term *call* is never referred to in the list of qualifications for church leadership in 1 Timothy 3 or Titus 1.

What are the possible implications of using terms such as, "I'm called to the XYZ mission society or organization"? Is there a better way to communicate that idea?

_____

_____

_____

Where are we then and what do we mean by the call? For many the traditional use of call relates to a feeling or conviction that they should be in a particular country or in a certain kind of ministry. The call is tied to God's guidance for special service, usually in the cross-cultural sense. One should never go out without one, for that would be inviting trouble. Ignoring the call would be disobedience and result in serious consequences and loss. The call usually comes through the formula of the Word, prayer and circumstances.

On the other hand, a number of Bible teachers or mission leaders question the biblical validity of a special missionary call. They stress Scripture's commands to go and make disciples are evident, and extraordinary guidance of a subjective nature is unnecessary. Their emphasis is on a person's suitability and availability to respond to given needs or opportunities. If those are in tandem from an objective standpoint, the person should move ahead even without a "feeling" of being called.

Between these two idealized poles is the use by many of the term "call" in a generic sense, synonymous with God's guidance, including both subjective and objective factors. Although in this system an individual's convictions are given consideration, responsibility for assessing suitability is not ignored. If the qualifications are lacking, the church or mission agency usually discourage candidacy, regardless of the person's subjective feelings.

To tie these things together and put things into perspective, answer the following questions:

On what basis did Paul choose Silas as his missionary colleague? See what you can deduce from Acts 15:22, 32.

_____

_____

_____

_____

Did Silas' qualifications include a "call"?

_____

_____

What was involved in the selection of Timothy as a missionary? See Acts 16:1-3.

_____

_____

When a person desires to be a church leader as expressed in I Timothy 3:1, is he automatically allowed to?

_____

_____

What qualifications are required? See 1 Timothy 3:2-7.

_____

_____

What are the implications then for someone wanting to become a missionary? Is a sense of call enough?

_____

_____

SUITABILITY FOR MISSIONS

Even if there is no neat formula for determining whether a particular person should go cross-culturally, there are some guidelines.

Are we left to our own devices and common sense? No, the Bible clearly outlines the principles and provides man illustrations of how God leads his people into positions and places of effective and fruitful ministry. We aren't left to mere human reasons for making career decisions.

Before I mention further details on guidelines, let

me re-emphasize a fundamental point. It's easy to limit world evangelization to a specialized task, delegated to an elite corps of bionic Christians, drafted to that order by a "call" few receive. In that process we lose sight of the general call of God for world evangelization to the entire church and not just a select few. No believer is exempt from the Great Commission on the grounds that he or she has not received a specific "call," any more than any Christian is free not to love his neighbor because of the lack of a personalized command. There is no dichotomy in God's program, no personal preference for involvement in world missions. In this sense we are all called to global evangelization.

Let's look at the suitability factors for guidance in missions. This should be the starting point in asking the question, "Does God want me on the mission field?"

1. **Recognition of gifts.** Any realistic assessment of suitability for missions must take into account one's spiritual gifts. Good intentions and willingness to go anywhere, while commendable, are not enough. A close look at Paul's selection criteria for his missionary team in Acts 15 and 16 shows that his focus was on giftedness, character and proven performance. Nothing is said about a call to missionary service or even if the individual felt "led." From the New Testament patterns, it's safe to say that the church's recognition of gifts and suitability is highly impor-

tant in the decision-making process.

What gifts are crucial to functioning effectively cross-culturally? How do you know if you have them?

_____

_____

_____

_____

If you feel you need additional help in understanding spiritual gifts, or in discovering the gifts you have, check with your church leaders for recommendations on resources your church uses in this area.

Some feel the so-called missionary call is in reality a spiritual gift—that is, the capacity to utilize one's gifts in a cross-cultural context. Therefore to have the gift is to have the call, as they are integrally related. A basis for this may be found in Paul's expression "grace to be a minister to the Gentiles," which he frequently uses not only in the sense of privilege but also with the sense of capacity or ability.

Check out Ephesians 3:8; Romans 15:15-16. Is there a connection with cross-cultural ministry? What is it?

_____

_____

At any rate, experience proves that not everyone is able to function effectively in cross-cultural living situations. Whether the capacity to communicate, adapt, and function is a "missionary gift" or a combination of natural skills or abilities, which are part of God's sovereign preparation of the individual, the end result is probably the same.

One thing is clear: the would-be missionary should demonstrate the ability to minister effectively on the basis of gifts at home before making serious plans to go elsewhere. The best place for the presence of gifts to be seen is within the Body of Christ. Confirmation by other mature and spiritual believers is an essential step in affirming a direction towards missionary service.

2. **Interpersonal skills.** Most failures in missionary service stem from relationships. The ability to relate to other mission and national colleagues is crucial. Building positive interpersonal skills starts with a biblical perspective on one's self-worth, abilities, weaknesses, strengths, and acceptance of basic temperament and personality. Without a healthy self-image and a right sense of self-esteem, relational or emotional complications are likely.

In Paul's list of leadership qualities in 1 Timothy 3 and Titus 1, are any emphasized over the others?

_____

_____

_____

_____

_____

Missionary effectiveness hinges on the ability to build and maintain wholesome relationships. More and more mission agencies are aware of this. Many have increased their screening efforts to insure candidates have the necessary people skills, as well as the technical.

3. **Communication skills.** Working in a different language and culture demands certain basic skills along with right attitudes. How well you communicate at home can be an indication of how well you will communicate overseas. What kind of feedback from church leaders, friends, or teachers have you received as to how you get your points across in teaching or speaking?

4. **Spiritual maturity and experience.** The mission field is no place for a spiritual novice. It is crucial to have proved God at home, in life and ministry

before assuming you are ready to serve elsewhere. A pattern of personal devotions, awareness of the spiritual battle, evidence of fruitfulness and effectiveness in ministry are tools of the trade and should be recognized in your life.

5 **Training and preparation.** It is generally true that a call to service is also a call to preparation. For instance, pioneer church planting is one of the most demanding roles in life. It requires a good foundation in general education, Bible knowledge, theology and missiology. A period of secular work is as important as experience in ministry. Many people come into missions having had little interaction with the rough and tumble of the marketplace and secular life. Can you maintain a consistent Christian life in secular surroundings? Before going overseas, get experience in work where your theology and classroom work are thoroughly tested and proved.

MEASURING UP

A study by Richard and Barbara Hawthorne of Wycliffe Bible Translators on the personality qualities which help people function effectively cross-culturally turned up the following list. It's called the "Hardy Personality." Rate yourself on a scale of 1-6. If the statement is very true of you, give yourself a 6, if it isn't true of you at all, give yourself a 1.

Hardy Personality Rating

Circle the appropriate figure:

1. I accept pain and pleasure as both
   part of life.   1 2 3 4 5 6

2. I am able to handle deprivation—
   going without won't kill me!   1 2 3 4 5 6

3. I am not given to addictions
   (no need for highs).   1 2 3 4 5 6

4. I have a positive attitude towards
   control (not demanding or abdicating). 1 2 3 4 5 6

5. I have a healthy perspective of myself
   (I'm in the story, not the whole story).   1 2 3 4 5 6

6. I have balanced self-knowledge
   (non-defensive and non-preoccupied).   1 2 3 4 5 6

7. I am able to accept responsibility
   without blaming.   1 2 3 4 5 6

8. I am able to give (love, energy, resources
   and time) and am not just a hoarder.   1 2 3 4 5 6

9. I have a sense of hope and basic
   optimism (the game isn't over until the
   last out has been made).   1 2 3 4 5 6

10. I'm my own bottom line (positive,
    not whining, passive, helpless or
    overly dependent).   1 2 3 4 5 6

11. I am able to use parts (innovative,
    creative, able to conceptualize, use
    what there is).   1 2 3 4 5 6

12. I am free to enjoy second choices

(not pouting or controlled by
disappointment).   1 2 3 4 5 6
13. I have a sense of humor and don't
take myself too seriously (flexible, free,
able to enjoy things).   1 2 3 4 5 6
14. I am able to restart (pick up after
failure, rebuff or rejection).   1 2 3 4 5 6

If the majority of your scores were to the right side of the graph, consider your personality "hardy." If the majority of your scores were to the left, you should work to develop these areas.

Feeling overwhelmed? Mission boards don't really expect perfect people. What is important is the direction you're heading and your willingness to learn, adapt and grow. When we look at the attrition rate in missions and the casualties from people returning home prematurely, we see the importance of careful screening. Your long-term welfare is at stake here. In a recent study of why missionaries leave the field, the top two reasons given were 1) lack of a sense of progress in the work, and 2) a sense of not having the right gifts and skills for the work that needs to be done.

What are your greatest fears in this area? List them briefly, then discuss them with your church leaders and key individuals who will pray through them with you.

_____

_____

_____

_____

Here are some questions any mission board is likely to ask you in weighing your suitability:

1. How well do you know God?

_____

2. How real is your sense of call?

_____

_____

3. Have you ever accomplished anything? What?

_____

_____

_____

4. Have you ever begun anything new? What?

_____

_____

_____

5. What can you contribute?

_____

_____

_____

6. Can you work in a team? How do you know?

_____

_____

7. Can you work with people different from yourself?

_____

8. What signs of self-discipline are evident in your life?

_____

_____

9. Do you listen well?

_____

10. Do people seek you out for friendship and counsel?

_____

11. Do you communicate clearly?

_____

12. Do you know how to disciple someone?

_____

13. Do you understand the dynamics of church life?

_____

14. Do you have language motivation?

_____

15. Are you ready to abandon national and ethnic pride?

_____

_____

Suitability is a factor considered not only by the sending church and agency, but also the national, receiving church and the immigration office of the host country. As a growing number of nations are defining and limiting the kinds of people they will accept into their country on missionary (or other) visas, suitability must be taken seriously and will not be left to the subjective perspective of a would-be missionary.

Feeling a bit inadequate or unworthy? All these lists and qualifications put our weaknesses in the spotlight.

Honest assessments can make us very insecure. Ironically, some have even found missionary biographies more of a hindrance than a help! Who can match the deeds of a William Carey, Hudson Taylor or Adoniram Judson?

Our weakness alone shouldn't paralyze us from obedience. The Apostle Paul himself, as a pioneer church planter in Corinth, could confess, "I came to you in weakness and fear, and with much trembling" (1 Cor. 2:3). But Paul didn't look to his own adequacy but to the infinite resources of the God who was with him.

All missionaries sometimes feel overwhelmed, inadequate or fearful. The demands are daunting and the obstacles formidable. At the same time, God must be our adequacy wherever we are (2 Cor. 3:5-6). Remember the words of Hudson Taylor, "All God's giants have been weak men, who did great things because they reckoned on his being with them."

IF I DON'T GO, THEN WHAT?

If I don't "feel called" or am assessed as "unsuitable" for cross-cultural missionary service does that mean I'm off the hook and can just forget about missions? Hardly! The Great Commission was given to the whole church and not just to an elite few. Not everyone can or should go, but all of us need to somehow partner in the Great Commission process as a sender. The sending part of the missions enterprise is equally vital and without people praying, giving, supporting and mobilizing on behalf of missions, the outreach of missions would soon wither and fade. Being a sender is far from a "second class" contribution to the global missions.

A quick look at the church in Philippi will give some indication of how we can contribute to missions in a variety of important ways in keeping with our particular gifts, resources and opportunities. The Apostle Paul described these believers as "partners in the gospel" (Phil. 1:5). They were all called to "live a life worthy of the gospel" (1:27) and through this lifestyle give credibility to the gospel claims. In addition Paul saw them contributing through prayer (1:19), facilitating the sending of workers (2:25), providing pastoral care to missionaries (4:10), and sharing generously their resources to support missionary work (4:14-16). That's quite a model for all of us to follow regardless of whether we go or stay.

It is also important to keep in mind that a vital role of the "sender" is mobilizing for the cause of missions. In other words, playing a part in creating missions awareness, interest, concern and then helping individuals find ways to contribute or support missionary efforts. The following diagram may help you better understand the overall process of mobilizing people and resources for missions and clarify how you can encourage individuals or churches to move from apathy or ignorance to some form of vital partnership in missions.

Process—Stages in Becoming a Global Christian
1. Initial exposure
2. Biblical and global awareness
3. Vision of what can be done
4. General commitment to do something
5. Specific commitment to a particular ministry
6. Strategic involvement (go, send, mobilize)

Global
Christian

As you look at this continuum of involvement, in what

ways do you think you could contribute to the mobilization process, whether you are going or staying?

_____

_____

_____

_____

_____

_____

_____

_____

8

praying for missions—
the best place to begin

everal years ago at the close of a missions meeting where I had stressed the need of prayer for missions, a frustrated man confronted me. "Why do missionaries need so much prayer? What's their problem? Can't they pray for themselves? I don't go around pleading for prayer for myself, and I live and work in a tough situation. Why are missionaries so needy that I should spend all my time praying for them?!"

Though I was surprised by his confrontation, I appreciated his honesty. It's a good question. Why should we pray for missions, and why is it important for you to begin praying regularly and earnestly now?

Before we try to answer these questions, let's begin this study with a quiz. Let's call it the MIQ (Missions Involvement Quotient).

MISSIONS INVOLVEMENT QUOTIENT

Please answer the following as best you can.

		Yes	No
1.	I can name two missionaries my church supports.	❏	❏
2.	I have read their latest prayer letters.	❏	❏
3.	I can list at least two prayer items requested by them recently.	❏	❏
4.	I am praying regularly for an unreached people group.	❏	❏
5.	I am using prayer material from at least one mission agency on a regular basis.	❏	❏
6.	I pray for the mission requests in the church bulletin.	❏	❏
7.	I am reading and using *Operation World* or other resource for prayer.	❏	❏
8.	I attend prayer meeting at church regularly.	❏	❏
9.	I'm involved with a missions prayer group or prayer partner.	❏	❏
10.	I turn news items on world concerns into prayer.	❏	❏

Well, how's your MIQ? If you scored low, hopefully you'll get the message that prayer and missions go together! If you hope others will pray for you when you're a missionary, you need to start the process yourself.

Most of us give lip service to the importance and priority of prayer, but a long, honest look at our actual performance often indicates a gap between what we say we believe and what we really believe. While our focus here is on prayer for missions we fully realize that we are called upon to pray for many other areas and needs which are equally important. Prayer for missions need not occupy all of our energy. It is not that praying for missions is more "spiritual" than other categories, but reality shows us that all too often what is out of sight is often out of mind! Thus without intentionality and commitment, prayer for missions can easily get dropped from our lists.

WHY PRAY FOR MISSIONS?

Let's look at what makes prayer for missions so vital. Without a solid biblical basis, we can easily lose our fervency and faithfulness in this critical ministry.

Partnership in ministry. In Romans 15:30-32 we see the Apostle Paul pleading with the Christians in Rome to pray for him. How strong is Paul's appeal?

_____

Why do you think Paul needs or wants their prayer participation?

_____

_____

For what does Paul request prayer?

_____

_____

_____

What does this imply for us in praying for missionaries?

_____

_____

_____

Apparently the Apostle Paul is calling these believers in Rome to have a part in his ministry through prayer. The imagery of "join me in my struggle by praying" is the idea of a Greek game with teams on a playing field. Paul looks up and realizes he is vastly outnumbered by his opponents, and looks to the bench for others to join him. Prayer for missions is God's way of giving us opportunities to join a ministry team—to become part of what he is doing through the work of another.

Isn't that fantastic? Just imagine! We can multiply and extend our ministries worldwide by praying!

Along the same line, check out Philippians 1:19. What is Paul assuming these Christians will do on his behalf?

_____

_____

_____

_____

What is the connection between Paul's circumstances and the prayers of these Philippians?

_____

_____

Why is God dependent upon our prayers to do his work of deliverance?

_____

_____

Therefore God calls us to pray for missions as a way of becoming prayer partners in his work in this world.

Power and protection in ministry. 2 Corinthians 1:10-11 reveals additional insights as to why prayer for missionaries and their work is so important.

Whom does Paul credit for his recent deliverance?

_____

_____

As he looks ahead to future deliverance from perils, what part will these Corinthian believers play?

_____

_____

What's the rationale for having many persons praying on Paul's behalf? (v.11)

It's amazing that God limits his work to our cooperation. While God is certainly capable of acting without our prayers, he chooses to use human means in accomplishing his work; in this case, it involves prayer. We could say the same thing about God's use of people in evangelism to bring the lost to Christ. He could use angels or other non-human means, but God deliberately chooses people to accomplish some of his purposes.

That's how it is with prayer. We don't fully understand why God waits to act until we pray, but he uses our prayers as part of a sovereign plan.

Open doors for ministry. Look at Colossians 4:2-4. How seriously should we take prayer?

_____

_____

What is the connection between prayer and opportunities for the gospel?

_____

_____

To what extent was Paul dependent upon the Colossian believers for effectiveness in his work?

_____

It's awesome to consider that individuals and local churches have the key to open doors for the gospel worldwide right within our grasp! Prayer is pictured as a key that opens doors. Are you using your key as you should?

Propel laborers into the harvest. Look at Luke 10:2 and Matthew 9:38. How do we recruit new workers?

Why is it necessary to pray for workers?

The people in today's world aren't just in need of missionaries, but God-sent ones. Hudson Taylor was compelled by this need years ago: "In the study of that divine Word I learned that to obtain successful laborers, not elaborate appeals for help, but first earnest prayer to God to thrust forth laborers and, second, the deepening of the spiritual life of the church so that men should be unable to stay at home were what was needed."

Does prayer make a difference in world evangelization? The above passages speak for themselves. Arnold Geswein also underscored the truth of Scripture when he stated, "Do not expect God to do, apart from prayer, what he has said he would do only if we pray."

Also don't forget your need to prove the faithfulness of God in answered prayer before you move into cross-cultural ministry. If you're not yet convinced that God hears and answers prayer at home, don't expect to believe it on the field. Hudson Taylor began preparing for work in China in his late teens. At that time (the early 1850s) there was very little support structures for a missionary in China, not to mention the harsh living conditions there. He wrote later in his biography, "When I get out to China, I thought to myself, I shall have no claim on anyone for anything. My only claim will be on God. How important to learn before leaving England, to move man through God by prayer alone!"

What's in it for me? As we have seen above, praying for God's global concerns not only contributes to God's purposes and the effectiveness of missionary ministry, but prayer offers something to us as well. Prayer obviously helps the missionary you pray for, but what can you gain from praying for someone else?

- By praying for global missions we actually can become partners with God and those missionaries. What a tremendous privilege to be a genuine part of something so significant and of eternal value.
- We can extend our ministry all around the world by

praying. It means that we are not shut up to just our immediate context but can actually serve unseen in people's lives and needs in all parts of the world.

- We ourselves can be encouraged and strengthened by what we see God doing in the lives of others elsewhere as we pray for them. We realize afresh that what God can do for others he can do for us.

- Regardless of our personal gifting, educational background, age, health condition or personal circumstances, we can touch other peoples' lives through prayer. There are no limitations or special requirements to be a prayer partner. What an incredible privilege and joy.

BEING AN EFFECTIVE PRAYER PARTNER

Let's get practical about prayer for missionaries. How can you develop your prayer life and encourage others to pray effectively for missionaries you know? Bill Wilson of OMF International has written a very helpful guide. Let's look at his suggestions:

1. **Maintain a broad general interest in missions around the world.** Pray for as many missionaries and for God's work in various countries as you can. Include your church's missionaries, and roam the world with your prayer support. You may want to set a schedule to pray for one missionary each day of the month. You may wish to focus your concern

on a different continent each day of the week. Operation Mobilization has excellent materials to help you in your prayer ministry worldwide. I recommend the following:

■ Pray-for-the-World Map—a good, large up-to-date world map.

■ *Operation World*—this book gives brief information and prayer requests for all the countries of the world.

■ Pack of cards—giving brief information and prayer requests for 68 spiritually needy nations. You may purchase the above items from STL Publications, P.O. Box 28, Waynesboro, GA 30830.

2. **Get deeply involved in praying regularly for one missionary or a missionary family.** Focus your burden on one particular outreach or ministry. Ask God to lay one specific missionary on your heart and determine to get involved with that missionary in a deep, meaningful way. We might say, adopt a missionary. Commit yourself to daily prayer and ask God to give you faithfulness in this ministry.

You'll want to learn all you can about this missionary; the family, mission agency, field strategy, the conditions of the country, type of work etc. Write them for further information. Ask to be put on their mailing list for prayer letters. Pray through those letters as carefully as you'd like close friends to pray for you.

But let's face it. Some missionaries don't write regularly or with enough prayer fuel. What then? Here is a daily routine with prayer topics that Bill Wilson suggests:

Day 1. Your missionary's own relationship to God. Don't assume they are always "on top" spiritually. Pray that he or she will feed on God's Word and pray regularly, not allowing a busy schedule to squeeze out this crucial activity. Pray they may be filled with the Spirit and grow in maturity and grace, with true victory over temptation, sin and Satan.

Day 2. Your missionary's physical and emotional life. Many missionaries work in difficult places where diseases and dangers are prevalent. Pray for safety. They also need emotional balance in the pressures and demands of cross-cultural living. Pray especially for deliverance from discouragement, loneliness and depression.

Day 3. Your missionary's family. The pressure on a husband and wife along with their children can be considerable on the mission field. Remember their needs for good communication and quality times together. Pray for their adjustment and adequate provision for schooling needs. Pray their family might model to others what a Christian home should be. If your missionary is single, pray for the special concerns that brings.

Day 4. Your missionary's ability to communicate. In missionary work communication is the essential factor. They are there to proclaim Christ. While lifestyle is essential, good language ability is also a must. Pray for adequate language study, sensitivity to culture and appropriate communication within it. Finally, ask for boldness to proclaim Christ when opportunities arise.

Day 5. Your missionary's ministry. It is important to pray for your missionary's work needs and goals. Prayer must be brought to bear on the area of daily activities and opportunities for witnessing, teaching and other forms of outreach. Pray your missionary will be empowered by the Holy Spirit for fruitful and effective service.

Day 6. Your missionary's fellow workers. Relationships can be both a tremendous strength and a point of tension. Satan often focuses his attacks in this area, so it's important to pray for unity, graciousness and forgiveness in the various working relationships between your missionary and his colleagues. Pray for teamwork and like-mindedness.

Day 7. Your missionary's country of service. Paul makes it clear in 1 Timothy 2:1 that prayer should be offered up for political governments since the progress of the gospel is greatly affected by the attitudes and actions of the state. Remember the need for visas, required for residence in most countries. Pray for a favorable attitude on the part of the state towards the work of missionaries. Ask God for a climate of peace in which the church can grow without hindrances or persecution.

PRAYER TOOLS AND RESOURCES

There is an amazing amount of resources to help you pray intelligently and faithfully. Let me itemize a few:

Books—Many of these are classics and can be obtained online or through your local Christian bookstore.

Prayer Power Unlimited, J.O. Sanders, Moody Press.

Touch The World Through Prayer, Wesley Duewel, Zondervan.

No Easy Road, Dick Eastman, Baker Books.

All Things Are Possible Through Prayer, Charles Allen, Spire.

Pray in the Spirit, Arthur Wallis, Christian Literature Crusade.

The Power of Prayer, R.A. Torrey, Zondervan.

With Christ in the School of Prayer, Andrew Murray, Spire.

Born for Battle, Arthur Mathews, OMF Books.

With Concerts of Prayer, David Bryant, Regal Books.

Pamphlets

7 Ways to Pray for Your Missionary, OMF, Littleton.

Why and How to Pray for Missionaries, OMF, Littleton.

Specialized Prayer Newsletters
Global Chinese Ministries, OMF.
Global Prayer Digest, U.S. Center for World Missions.
Fellowship of Faith for Muslims.

Now then let's turn the above into an action plan. What will you do in terms of personal prayer and study?

I will read the following books: _____

_____

_____

I will begin praying for the following missionaries:

_____

_____

_____

I will use the following prayer resources regularly:

_____

_____

_____

I am asking God to help me pray in the following way:

_____

_____

_____

DOING IT TOGETHER

Recognizing we all find it hard to stick at a task alone, I encourage you to start a missions prayer group if one is not available to you. It only requires a commitment to pray regularly and a realization of the mutual benefits. Here are some suggestions to get something launched:

1. **Getting started**
   - Fix a time and place whether in a home or at church.
   - Meet regularly as this provides more stable attendance.
   - Tie the meeting in with other events to avoid conflicts.

2. **Structuring the meeting**
   - Appoint a leader who can facilitate the meeting.
   - Limit the time to about one hour.
   - Major on prayer, not just information about prayer.
   - Have letters or handouts prepared ahead of time.

3. **Praying**
   - Limit the scope of your praying to not overwhelm people. Start with a few missionaries and situations, then add others as members can handle it.
   - Pray for specific needs and requests.

- Don't forget praise and thanksgiving as well.
- Follow up on prayer requests to see how they are answered.

Occasionally special prayer events can be planned for a local church that can be of tremendous blessing. Consider a Concert of Prayer for a Saturday, or even a prayer vigil on a Friday night. Some mission agencies such as OMF offer weekend prayer conferences to focus prayer on Asia and other areas.

I'm reminded again in 1 Timothy 2:1-8 that God sees prayer as the first priority within the ministry of the local church. Why? Paul asserts that prayer for all affects the progress of the gospel and the welfare of the Christian community (v.2). Prayer for all is consistent with the very plan of God, who desires all men to be saved. There is only one mediator for all (v.5), one ransom for all (v.6), and one message for all (v.7). Based on these tremendous truths, the apostle pleads, "I want men everywhere to lift up holy hands in prayer, without anger and disputing" (v.8).

What practical things can you learn about prayer in 1 Timothy 2:1-8?

_____

_____

_____

_____

The history of missions shows an inextricable link between prayer and the progress of the gospel. To see spiritual progress in the 21st century, God's people must make prayer the first priority. In the words of the missionary statesman, the late Robert E. Speer: "The evangelization of the world in this generation depends first of all upon a revival of prayer. Deeper than the need for men, deeper than the need for money; deep down at the bottom of our spiritless life is the need for the forgotten secret of prevailing, worldwide prayer." There is no greater work, no greater priority, than the work of the church on her knees.

Look back at the Missions Involvement Quiz you took at the beginning of this chapter. Write out a prayer to God asking him to help you change at least two of your "no" answers (if you had any) to "yes" within the next month.

9

finding the right track

Want to get confused? Try writing ten different mission agencies asking for information on the kind of programs they offer for summer, short-term and long-term service. After the mail truck unloads all the replies, settle back for a month or two to read your way through it. If you last long enough you'll discover no shortage of mission programs or tracks. How then do you sort out what might be best for you and where to start?

Let's begin by going back to the basic things we mentioned earlier about consulting with your home church about your decisions. It is quite likely the missions committee has already done some homework and has some recommendations for you. You may be a part of a Christian campus ministry which has various summer or career programs to offer, and they might also help in sorting out preferable options. Again, make choices with your local church in view, so you don't end up picking programs that do not fit into their strategy or program.

SUMMER PROGRAMS

An increasing number of young people are investing a summer in a missions program. Today 90 percent of career missionaries have had some kind of short-term missions experience. There are a number of advantages and benefits:

1. It offers you a first-hand taste of what cross-cultural life is all about.
2. Provides an objective basis to determine if your gifts, skills and temperament suit missionary work.
3. Indicates the kind of further training and preparation which would be most helpful to you.
4. Can help build Christian character and maturity.
5. Broadens vision and world awareness for yourself, your church and friends at home.
6. It serves as an outlet for you to contribute directly to field projects, ministries and morale.

Keep in mind that summer programs or short-term mission projects do have their drawbacks or limitations:

1. A short exposure to a field may be uncharacteristically negative or unrealistically positive. Either way, it may not be an adequate basis to make long-term

decisions for career involvement. In other words, a brief time on the field may be fun but fail to give a full picture of what mission life is really like. Most summer workers never face the shocks and strains of language study, cultural adjustments and ministry pressures.

2. Short-term programs may be expensive and your involvement may not really contribute to personal or strategic goals. While there is a certain value to anyone traveling cross-culturally, unfortunately, too many go out more as tourists and adventurers rather than as ministers. However, it is probably in your best interest to spend 6-8 weeks in a summer/short-term mission program. The following suggestions can guide you in some of the decisions you need to make:

   ■ Talk over options with your missions committee/pastor.

   ■ Compare programs with agencies in terms of costs, objectives and requirements. Not all are of equal value.

   ■ Go with a team from your church if possible.

   ■ Plan well in advance for preparation, passport/visa requirements and support-raising. Start the application process early.

   ■ Recruit a group of prayer partners.

   ■ Inquire about ways of presenting your program

to the church both before and after the trip.

- Don't be swayed by the glamour of exotic places, as a domestic inner-city program may be an equal or better value for experience and less expensive.
- Be realistic about your summer expectations. The trip will probably benefit you more than the field you will be serving.

If you are considering a summer missions trip (or know someone who is), make a list of prayer requests based on the suggestions you've just read.

_____

_____

_____

_____

_____

_____

If you've already taken a summer trip, list prayer requests to help you implement what you gained from that ministry into your life. Did you set goals you've not followed through on? Have you forgotten things that should still be important to you? Is there any "unfinished business" you should be taking care of?

_____

_____

_____

How may a short-term experience prepare your church if you should later decide to go into career missions?

_____

_____

_____

_____

_____

SHORT-TERM PROGRAMS

Normally any period from a few weeks to four years is considered short term. For our purposes, we'll view programs from one to four years as short term. A number of mission agencies specialize in short-term programs, but most traditional agencies have short-term options too.

What are some of the advantages of involvement in a short-term program?

- A realistic view of missions before making a career decision.

- Your skills and services can meet vital field needs and free field personnel for other tasks.

- Gives you experience to bring back to your local church for their mission vision and growth. Helps you keep in mind some of the limitations or dangers.

Short-term involvement normally has limitations in the amount of time available for language acquisition and cultural integration. This can make your time rather frustrating. Also a short-term stint should not be seen as a substitute for career availability if God is calling you to that. Some feel if they give God a couple of years overseas, they've "put in their time" and are off the hook for further responsibility to world missions. Others use it as a way of making their resume look good. Thus motives for considering short-term service need to be honestly thought through. I also advise careful consultation with your pastor or other Christian leaders.

MISSIONARY OR TENTMAKER

In considering career missions or even short-term missions, you'll have to decide between the traditional role as a supported missionary or a Christian professional, also called a tentmaker. What issues are involved? Which is right for you?

Perhaps before we go further it might be helpful to clarify just what we mean by "tentmaker." According to Don Hamilton in the very helpful resource book on tentmaking entitled, *Working Your Way to the Nations: A Guide to Effective Tentmaking*, a tentmaker is defined as a Christian who works in a cross-cultural situation, is recognized by members of the host culture as something other than a "religious professional," and yet, in terms of their commitment, calling, motivation and training, is a "missionary" in every way.

Ian Prescott of OMF International adds this important note, "Our Professional Service Associates (tentmakers) are genuinely not missionaries in the sense in which most governments define missionaries—full-time religious workers. However, they are missionaries in a much more important theological sense—those who have been sent; who in response to God's call, have deliberately crossed cultural barriers with the specific intent of witness to Christ. They are not simply professionals pursuing their vocation in another country and taking the opportunity to witness. They are individuals who have responded to a calling from God to contribute to the establishment and growth of the church in another country and culture—using their professional skills to enable them to do these things."

In the geo-political arena of our world today, not every country is open to traditional missionaries. Nations that limit or forbid formal missionary work are known as limited-access nations. Actually I like the term creative-access nation better, as it doesn't imply any limits to what God can do. Countries that allow missionary work are known as open-access nations.

At present there is a considerable variety of roles in which you can function as a missionary, although your label may vary. The traditional role is the full-time evangelist/church-planter, discipler, theological educator, etc. Many countries are open to these personnel, although an increasing number have laid down certain visa requirements and qualifications.

A large number of the major unreached people groups, however, are found in creative-access countries. Although we use the term "creative access" we don't want to give the impression, however, that one needs to be highly inventive to gain access! The openings in most creative-access nations are many and various—they are just "not for missionaries." According to Ian Prescott, "The biggest challenge is not finding ways to get in, but finding people to go in!" To fulfill the Great Commission in these places, it is necessary for Christians to enter as professionals or work from a business or technical platform with marketable skills or as students. Actually, Christian professionals also function effectively in open-access countries, reaching some the traditional missionary might not.

Here is a summary of descriptions of Christians abroad to provide ideas for possible roles:

1. **On assignment.** Business, military, students or other professionals often have work that assigns them temporarily overseas. They may relate to local national churches or the missions community. Their ministry, however, is limited because of their purpose overseas, time, language or company requirements.

2. **As a Christian professional (tentmaker).** This person consciously chooses to serve overseas as a

Christian witness/church-planter where there are visa restrictions for regular missionaries or unique opportunities in a secular role. They usually see themselves as sent by a home church.

3. **As a professional service associate.** This person is working with a mission agency but serving in a secular appointment such as a teacher, consultant, medical specialist etc. Their placement is part of a strategy by the mission agency to gain access to certain kinds of people or unreached groups.

4. **Full-time missionary.** This is the traditional missionary who is sent and supported full-time for ministry abroad.

It is helpful to keep in mind that a tentmaker is more than a Christian living overseas. Technically a tentmaker is seen as a person who has:

- the right motivation
- adequate training
- is affiliated with church and agency
- is employed
- engages in ministry opportunity
- seeks strategic positions

At any rate, many factors should be considered in deciding your role in missions. I would recommend the study guide *Working Your Way to the Nations; A Guide to Effective Tentmaking* edited by Jonathan Lewis (InterVarsity Press, 1996) as a very helpful resource for thinking through what is involved in creative-access missions or tentmaking, and whether or not it best matches your gifts, skills, training, ministry expectations and personal qualifications.

Tentmaking is certainly not for everyone. Some have tended to romanticize it as the ideal way to serve cross-culturally in following the Great Commission. The hard reality is that many have started in this direction and yet have returned frustrated and disappointed. There are some highly qualified professionals who go overseas only to discover that there are limits to what they can do or how long they can remain in a role. Thus for some highly career-minded professions, they would be better off going as "long-term short-termers" than as residential workers for the long haul. At any rate, it is very important to investigate carefully the options, needs and opportunities available and to seek competent advise in planning your next step.

For help in determining where you might fit, use the following considerations compiled by Ben Draper of OMF as a check list. While some of the statements or questions would equally apply to those considering a "traditional missionary" assignment, they hopefully will highlight some of the critical issues involved.

1. Basic Considerations
❏   Participating in extending God's church is top priority for me and my family. (Because you are sure to face sacrifices and hardships in a professional

role overseas, you must be convinced of your personal priorities. Accomplishing God's purposes must be more important to you than your own ambitions. And making a success of national Christians will always need to have higher priority than your own success.)

❏ I believe I can be a more effective Christian helper in a secular career than I can in a professional religious one. The following factors apply:

   ❏ I have proven secular professional skill.

   ❏ I can adjust to a different lifestyle.

   ❏ I have relational skills.

   ❏ Financially I prefer to support myself.

   ❏ My family and personal background fits the role of a professional overseas.

   ❏ I have theological training.

   ❏ I have ministry experience.

   ❏ I want to fill openings and unmet needs that others cannot fill.

2. Professional placement

❏ There is a need overseas for foreign experts in the field(s) in which I am trained (management, engineering, science, medicine, English language, teaching, agriculture etc.).

❏ I have the training (master's degree or doctorate) and experience (two years or more of employment or teaching).

❑   I am aware of specific openings in the country of

_____

❑   I know of companies or schools that could place
    me overseas. (Once you discover a likely channel
    of service, get in touch with their personnel depart-
    ment for more information.)

3. Christian preparedness

❑   I feel strong in Bible and theological knowledge
    and am thus confident that I am ready to witness
    as a layman overseas. (If you could not respond
    positively to this one, take time to seriously con-
    sider further biblical training. Many Bible colleges
    and seminaries offer special intensive courses to
    help prepare Christian professionals.)

❑   God has already used my witness and discipling
    ministry here at home in such a way that I feel sure
    he can use me in another country. (Substantial
    involvement in a local congregation or para-church
    ministry develops lay ministry skills such as teach-
    ing, friendship evangelism, counseling, small-
    group leadership—all of which are needed over-
    seas. Effective experience along this line is essential
    for a Christian professional headed overseas.)

❑   The leaders of my home congregation have
    acknowledged my sense of calling to overseas wit-
    ness and recognize that my ministry skills are com-
    patible. (The backing of a home church, especially

in prayer and in confirming your guidance, is essential. It is wise to discuss these things openly and prayerfully before moving ahead.)

❏ I am in touch with a mission or church agency with whose work I could cooperate. (Most missions welcome the cooperation of Christian professionals overseas.)

4. Personal factors

❏ My family responsibilities are such that I am able to live away from home for long periods of time. (Consider obligations to dependents and to parents, children's schooling, medical needs, and financial demands, including debts. Consider whether members of your household are all able and happy to live in a foreign environment.)

❏ I have the flexibility of lifestyle and the ability at language learning to adjust to a long-term living and ministry situation in an unfamiliar cultural environment.

❏ I am medically fit for the stress of living and working overseas for long periods.

❏ My personality fits me for cross-cultural ministry. I consider myself warm, outgoing, and teachable for other's well-being. (Experience with international students or refugees in the home country provides the opportunity to measure this factor.)

If you are a Christian who is committed to the world-wide expansion of Christ's church and have secular qualifications welcomed by official, business and educational leaders overseas, you may be the person to penetrate one of these restricted-access areas with the gospel.

In weighing up the options and considering how God wants to best use you in cross-cultural ministry, it would be helpful to see some of the advantages and limitations of tentmaking:

Advantages

- Accessibility to creative-access nations
- Credibility of tentmaker
- Unique opportunities
- Financial viability
- Christian role-modeling

Limitations

- Restricted job placement
- Job/ministry time conflicts
- Duration tied to contract
- Identification problems
- Negative associations

Would you make a better full-time missionary or professional? Support your answer.

_____

_____

_____

_____

_____

CAREER GUIDANCE FOR MISSIONS

As we've already seen, there are multiple tracks to missionary service both long and short term. Each of us has to weigh up our

- background and training
- ministry gifts and desires
- sense of leading to people groups or geographic areas
- evaluation of potential contribution.

In today's world there is need and room for both traditional missionaries and professionals. To reach restricted-access countries or people-groups, a mission agency may play a facilitating role in finding job placement for the tentmaker and providing administrative and pastoral support.

Not everyone is cut out to be a tentmaker. A tentmaker spends a good part of his day in a professional role requiring high professional integrity. That means the tentmaker should be comfortable in their profession and find reasonable satisfaction from it. If your first love is preaching and teaching the Word, a restricted country with major limits on your public ministry may be an unbearable situation. Better stewardship of your gifts and abilities may be in ministry in an open-access country where you could function with freedom. The priority of missions today is to plant the church of Jesus Christ where he is not known. There is plenty of scope both in the restricted-access and open-access nations of the world for both kinds of missionaries.

How will sending churches need to change or adjust so that missionaries in professional roles can have proper prayer support?

_____

_____

_____

Do you think churches will pray for those they don't need to support financially?

_____

How can you encourage your church in this new area of world ministry?

_____

_____

What kinds of openings does this create for those called to a specific vocation?

_____

_____

10

finding the right mission agency

I'll never forget that lecture! Having just graduated from university and sensing God's leading to full-time Christian work, I found myself in Bible school. A missions introduction course was required for all students, and on one particular day we had a guest speaker. He told of his early experiences as a pioneer missionary to Alaska. We alternated between laughing and crying as he related one fascinating story after another. Then as he brought the lecture to its main purpose, this missionary went on to give us fifty reasons why you should not go out as an independent missionary.

Obviously I got his point. I've never really considered serving overseas apart from a mission agency. I realize not everyone has had the benefit of that same lecture, and that circumstances don't dictate association with an agency as a must for everyone. Yet it's important to think through the implications of being an independent missionary versus being related to an agency.

OPTIONS

It is always helpful to think through the advantages and disadvantages in the choices we make. Let's think through the pros and cons of going overseas independently. First list the pros, then the cons:

Pros

_____

_____

_____

_____

_____

_____

Cons

_____

_____

_____

_____

_____

At heart are the issues of motives, security and qualifications. They need to be prayerfully examined.

Motives. Why am I going overseas independently?

What is my basic motivation? Some people are entrepreneurial in temperament and style. They just prefer to work independently. They don't like the restrictions and demands of an organization and function better as free agents. How justifiable is this in today's mission world?

_____

_____

_____

There are a number of independent missionaries around the world where working on one's own may be appropriate. If our primary motivation is a desire to not be held accountable, we have a serious problem. Scripture will give some clues to our interdependence and need for accountability to a body of believers. Look at Acts 13:3 and 14:26-28. What principles can be applied to the area of accountability?

_____

_____

_____

_____

_____

Check out also Paul's attitude in 2 Corinthians 8:18-21. What else can we learn?

_____

_____

_____

_____

_____

_____

Today's Christian public is looking for accountability in how resources are handled and spent through individuals, programs or agencies. At the same time, in our world of interconnectedness and networking, we need to be willing to cooperate with like-minded believers. The Lone Ranger mentality in missions is over.

Security. Working in a restricted-access nation may require special sensitivities to mission agency associations or labels. For instance, in the People's Republic of China, missionaries are not allowed to function. Any Christian going in to serve must have an identity different from "missionary." The same could be said for certain Islamic states where Christian activity is severely circumscribed or proscribed.

Therefore, some Christian professionals in these highly sensitive areas feel the only way to protect their status is to go independently. In talking with many in similar situations, there are still ways of associating with agencies to provide the kind of logistical, pastoral and accountability help all of us need. What are some of the benefits or problems for a person in this situation?

_____

_____

_____

_____

_____

_____

Requirements. Did you ever see the old movie, _Inn of the Sixth Happiness_? It's the story of Gladys Aylward whose life story was written in _The Small Woman_ and later made into a film. She applied to several mission boards in England, but was consistently turned down for service. She ended up going to China on her own. God honored her faith, and she served effectively there. There are instances when a person doesn't meet the qualifications of a mission board, yet still senses deeply a call to go; such a person sometimes ends up serving independently.

Do you feel this is a good and appropriate response when rejected by an agency?

_____

_____

_____

While Gladys Aylward's story had a happy ending, many other men and women have gone out against the advice of mature Christian workers and experienced painful consequences. We must be very careful in discerning when God is closing a door. I've also watched so-called independent missionaries flaunting their life of faith, and in reality they drew heavily from the resources and good will of other Christian workers on the field. Whether the Lord leads us to associate with an agency or not, we must realize our need for accountability and interdependence. We should also seek to be cooperative, as appropriate, with other parts of Christ's Body.

Before we go on, let me mention that a growing number of local churches are sending out their own missionaries and serving, in a sense, as their own sending agency. What do you feel are some of the strengths and weaknesses of this approach?

_____

_____

_____

_____

_____

Some churches have a strong base and missions vision along with adequate resources to enable them to function as their own agency. While there is much to commend in their close involvement with their missionaries, logistically there may be difficulties in providing the on-field support and strategic help normal mission agencies are equipped to provide. A basic question for the local church considering this approach is why duplicate what others are capably doing already? Are there no compatible agencies through which they can channel their missionaries? In a day of resource limitations and agency proliferation on the field, we need to be certain of our rationale before launching any new effort or organization.

WHAT TO LOOK FOR IN A MISSION AGENCY

I was advised as a missionary candidate to look carefully before committing myself to an agency. The imagery used was something akin to a marriage. Such a commitment drove me to know my future partner well, before walking the aisle! Other advice took a different angle. One advisor said with conviction, "It's more important to decide which team you want to play on than in which ball park." Choosing a suitable mission agency is like picking apples in a fruit salad. There are so many and it's not easy to see the difference from the outside. At present there are over 800 Protestant mission agencies working out of North America. How can you know which one is right for you? Here are some questions which should help you in the process of comparing and selecting a mission board. A good resource for helping you find out what boards are like is the *Mission Handbook: North American Protestant Ministries Overseas* published by MARC, Monrovia, CA.

Assignment: At this point, I suggest you contact three mission agencies. Make a separate file for each, enclosing their literature and your evaluation of them based on the following criteria. But before you start your evaluations read through the chapter and answer the questions so you know your own views.

Strategy

- What is the mission and vision of the agency?
- What are their core organizational values?
- What is their overall strategy?
- How does that strategy relate to your gifts and potential contribution?

Many agencies can be eliminated with this first question if they are involved in tasks and goals of secondary or no interest to you.

What types of ministry are you interested in? Is it based on geographical location or the task involved? How flexible are you in this area?

_____

_____

_____

Structure. Every organization is structured and administrated somewhat differently. It's helpful to have some idea of the agency's size and organizational pattern. Some agencies are really a Mom-and-Pop operation,

and others are very corporate in outlook and style.
Thus find out:

- The style of leadership.
- Is it democratic?
- Is it centralized?
- Is it field- or home-controlled?
- The degree of supervision, and accountability.

What type of leadership are you accustomed to working with?

_____

_____

What are the strengths of that method? What are its weaknesses?

_____

_____

_____

Ethos. Every agency is somewhat like a family. Some you're comfortable with; others you're glad to leave! The same is true for mission agencies as they are basically a product of the early leadership and forces that shaped their development. It's good to know the distinctives of the mission—its origin, founder and development. Some questions to ask:

- Is it a branch or split from another organization?

- What is the membership composition?
- Is it international?
- What are its church links and denominational leanings?

Financial Policy. Here's an area where it's helpful to do your homework. The fiscal functions of agencies vary, so careful research ahead of time will stand you in good stead. What are the implications of their stated financial policy?

- What are their deputation requirements?
- To what extent do they appeal for funds?
- What are their provisions and allowances for their personnel?
- As an agency are they a member of an accredited association such as the Interdenominational Foreign Missions Association, Evangelical Foreign Missions Association, Evangelical Council of Financial Accountability?

Define your personal philosophy for raising funds. Support it with scripture.

_____

_____

_____

_____

_____

Personnel Policy. How they process candidates and treat field personnel are critical areas to examine.

- What is expected of candidates?
- What are their qualifications and requirements for membership? (Remember that the easiest to get in to may not be the best.)
- Check their attitude towards families, children's education and the role of the wife.
- Do they have adequate orientation and language school programs?
- What do average members say about the organization as opposed to the leadership? Do they have a good reputation among the missions community?

List the qualifications and attitudes you feel to be most important. Does your church feel the same?

_____

_____

_____

_____

Relationships with National Churches. One of the best ways to find out the reputation and effectiveness of an agency is to ask a national familiar with their work on the field:

- What is the degree of identification, standard of living and lifestyle of their missionaries?

- With whom does the agency cooperate or not?
- What is their attitude toward international organizations such as WEF, WCC or national church associations?
- To what extent will they cooperate with other mission agencies or programs?

What type of lifestyle do you feel is most effective for missionaries?

_____

_____

List any organizations with whom you don't wish to be associated.

_____

_____

_____

Relationships with Home Churches. Another way of knowing what an agency is like is to look at its supporting constituency.
- What churches form its supporting constituency (independent, mainline denominational, Baptist, etc.)?
- Does it claim to be interdenominational?
- What are the promotional materials like?
- What degree of accountability to its supporters does it offer?

What are you expecting your mission board to do for your home church?

_____

_____

_____

_____

_____

Doctrinal Emphases. Here again it is important to look carefully at various boards. To be honest, most mission boards are evangelical, or they wouldn't still be in business! Within evangelical theology is a broad spectrum of exclusiveness, inclusiveness and tolerance towards others. Some mission boards were started as a reaction to a controversial issue and thus have a special doctrinal emphasis.

- What are the theological distinctives?
- Where do they draw the lines for inclusiveness?

Realize, too, there is more to a doctrinal statement than what is on paper. Try to discover what is emphasized or stressed.

What are some attitudes hidden in your own doctrinal statement?

_____

_____

_____

A number of new agencies have formed lately with a style somewhat different than traditional or older boards. We might call these contemporary agencies. They cater to the Generations X and Y values, needs and relational style. Some of these, however, may lack the proven stability and long-term track record important to consider.

What are the advantages of a contemporary board?

_____

_____

_____

What advantages can an older mission offer?

_____

_____

_____

SORTING THEM OUT

Let's go back to the previous mention of some 800 Protestant mission boards operating out of North America. Is it really necessary to go through each one with the above question grid? I can hear the groans! Not really. Mission agencies can be sorted into major categories to help you select more readily. The following may be helpful.

1. **Denominational or otherwise.** Many mission soci-

eties have strong evangelical denominations behind them. Even so, there is still a fair amount of variance in terms of denominational control. On the one hand, the Foreign Missions Board of the Southern Baptists and the Christian and Missionary Alliance would represent denominations with fairly strong influence on their mission boards. Other denominations such as the Evangelical Free Church of America support their own society, but local churches are free to support other groups as well. Most of the evangelical denominational societies belong to the Evangelical Fellowship of Mission Agencies (EFMA), a very helpful accrediting entity related to the National Association of Evangelicals and the World Evangelical Fellowship. It is important you understand where your home church stands and the boards they will endorse.

If your church won't support the mission you wish to join, should you switch churches or boards?

_____

_____

_____

2. **Affiliated or not.** As mentioned before, there are several accrediting associations of missions about which you should know. Whether or not a mission board belongs to one might be an important consid-

eration. Some churches, for instance, have a policy to only support missionaries with accredited agencies, such as the IFMA, EFMA or FOM.

3. **Task specific.** A number of agencies have come into being to focus on a specific task. Wycliffe Bible Translators is a good example of this kind of agency. Their priority, obviously, is the reduction of languages to writing and the production of Scriptures. Although Wycliffe needs all kinds of support people, their purpose is restricted.

4. **Geographically focused.** Many agencies originally came into being to reach a particular area of the world (China Inland Mission, Sudan Interior Mission, Africa Inland Mission). Even today only a select number of boards work worldwide, so your area of geographic interest will naturally eliminate some.

5. **Support/technical in function.** A number of agencies help evangelism/church-planting groups function better. In other words, they provide technical or support services. For instance, Mission Aviation Fellowship seeks to facilitate the transportation of missionaries to their assignments. Gospel Recordings, Inc. is designed to provide audio/visual recordings and equipment used in evangelistic outreach.

6. **International/domestic.** Many agencies are essentially North American. Some, however, have evolved into international agencies with an international headquarters outside North America.

7. **Tentmaker/traditional.** As mentioned before, several agencies today specialize in placing Christian professionals or tentmakers into overseas assignments. Some traditional boards (such as OMF or Interserve) combine both functions. Others are only equipped to work with traditional roles.

8. **Doctrinal orientation.** Another category of distinction is their charismatic or non-charismatic orientation. The number of charismatic churches in mission outreaches has grown significantly in recent years. The extent of your convictions in this area will direct you to specific agencies.

9. **Size.** It may sound strange to bring this factor in, but for some of us big is best, and others prefer to work in smaller groups. Agencies come in all sizes. Those considered to be very large, such as Wycliffe Bible Translators, YWAM and the Southern Baptist International Mission Board, have several thousand members. A medium or moderate size ranges from about 300 to 1,000 members. There are also very small agencies out there with only a handful of members.

Let me remind you that in looking for the "perfect" mission board we need to be realistic. Missions, like people, have their weaknesses, limits and failures. When in the application process to the OMF I was advised not to look just at what an agency could do for me, but also how God could use me to contribute and strengthen the agency. We have high expectations of churches and agencies, and rightfully so. The human element of any organization inevitably brings a certain amount of disappointment. If God leads you to an agency, trust him to enable you to work through the difficult times and still accomplish your ministry.

11

training and preparation
for missions

B y the time he finished, I was totally depressed! Could I ever match his expectations for a missionary? Listening to all the necessary preparation for overseas service left me ready to look into some other line of work.

Perhaps you haven't had this kind of experience, but mission representatives or furlough personnel often describe the ideal missionary in terms the Apostle Paul couldn't meet. They're only trying to be realistic about demands a missionary faces in cross-cultural ministry and want us to be as prepared as possible. How can we avoid extreme expectations or oversimplistic optimism? Let's think through these polarities.

WHAT WOULD YOU DO?
Scenario # 1
You've just arrived in a small, rural town of 40,000 pop-

ulation in northern Japan. This is your first assignment as a fledgling church planter. You've completed almost two years of full-time Japanese language study in another major center. The town is in an agricultural area producing rice and apples. The community is conservative, traditional and solidly Buddhist-Shinto.

The field plan is that you and your family reside in this city and seek to start a church. A nearby Japanese church sees this new work as desirable and wants to help within their limited resources. Another mission family lives 30 minutes away and should provide advice and fellowship. The Japanese Christian family in this town, promised to be the nucleus of the work, has just been transferred elsewhere, forcing you to start from scratch.

Don't forget—you're the first Protestant missionary to ever live here. Incidentally, there is one other church in town. It's small, Catholic and operates a kindergarten but has no resident priest. Their Mass services are attended by about five people on average.

How would you begin? What practical steps would you take to initiate contacts and work towards evangelizing this needy town and planting a church?

_____

_____

_____

_____

_____

Furthermore, if you knew this ministry was ahead of you, what preparation steps would you take (for the town and yourself)?

_____

_____

_____

_____

What kinds of skills or experience would be helpful or essential for a person in that particular situation?

_____

_____

_____

_____

_____

Scenario # 2

Imagine yourself in a restaurant in Hong Kong enjoying a delicious Chinese meal. You overhear a conversation among several waiters standing nearby. A reference is made to Christians and your immediate impression is that one of these restaurant workers is a believer. You engage him in conversation later, and discover he had used the term as a slang expression and has no interest in Christian things. In talking and checking further, you find he is one of thousands of waiters in Hong Kong. He and his colleagues are virtually cut off from any contact with church. The average waiter only has one day off every three weeks. His work hours almost prevent him from ever attending church services at their regular time.

As time goes by you have a growing burden for this unreached people group and feel you should reach them. How would you go about it? How would you find opportunities, particularly with their heavy work demands?

_____

_____

_____

_____

_____

If you were planning ahead for a ministry of this kind, what preparation do you think would be important?

_____

_____

_____

Again, what kind of skills would be helpful in reaching a group of people such as restaurant workers in urban Hong Kong?

_____

_____

_____

_____

Scenario # 3

As the speaker came to the close of his presentation on China, you felt challenged. "Could I possibly live and work in a place like China and there seek to share Christ?" you wonder. In talking with the speaker, you realize missionaries are not allowed in the country, but they welcome professional people who bring special skills and expertise to serve China's desperate efforts to modernize. You understand also that Chinese language study is important to function there long term. You will not be able to publicly preach and teach the gospel. Friendships and the outworking of a Christlike example in the workplace are the only opportunities for sharing Christ available to you.

In anticipating this kind of a ministry as a tentmaker, or Christian professional, how would you prepare and train? Also, what kind of skills would you need to be able to cope and function effectively in a restricted access country?

GUIDELINES FOR PREPARATION

Someone once said that a missionary could never be too prepared. God isn't asking us to be omni-competent before we can be useful to him. Your training and preparation will depend upon the kind of ministry you will assume and the related expectations. Technical and support roles demand skills that differ from a theological educator or church planter. We can break down preparation into several major categories that would apply to all potential missionaries.

1. **Development as a person and disciple of Jesus Christ.** The mission field is no place for the immature or spiritually naive. Therefore, part of preparation is learning to handle the responsibilities and demands of life where you are now. Maturity does not always equal age, so I'm not suggesting a time limit. I've seen very capable missionaries in their early twenties. In fact, Hudson Taylor sailed for China in 1853 when only 20 years old.

   Still, there is no substitute for time in growing and developing. A critical factor in maturing is how you handle opportunities, responsibilities and stress. These pressures will be multiplied in intensity on the mission field, so a certain amount of life testing needs to be done before you leave. Another litmus test of Christian maturity is faithfulness and obedience in the big or small details of life. Do you complete assignments or ministry responsibilities? Are you able to draw from God's spiritual resources to handle the decisions and demands of daily life? Have you proven God's power and provisions in times of special need?

2. **Development of ministry skills and spiritual gifts.** I'm fully convinced that when God calls, he also equips. He won't lead you to a task without providing the abilities to meet it. This is a process. We aren't fully functional as newborn Christians any more than we are as newborn infants!

How does the Apostle Paul encourage young Timothy as a developing pastor? Look carefully at 1 Timothy 4:11-16.

_____

_____

_____

_____

Later in 2 Timothy 1:6-7 Paul had to remind his disciple to develop further in what areas?

_____

_____

_____

It has been amazing to see how many missionary

candidates feel ready to go overseas once they have completed a course of studies. While these are helpful, they don't compare to proven ministry skills or gifts. Skills can best be developed in an internship arrangement through a local church or a program of a para-church organization. For many of you, a full-time position in Christian work for a year or two before actually going overseas can be extremely helpful preparation. Many mission boards require at least a year of full-time ministry.

A helpful rule in knowing if I am ready for a task is to ask the simple question of can I actually do it. Knowing how to preach is not the same as having actually preached. Studying evangelism in Bible school is good, but unless you have done it first hand it is impractical to think you're ready to train others.

3. **Biblical, theological and missiological education.** Again the time and formal study required in these areas varies according to mission board requirements and projected field responsibilities. The issue at heart is how well I grasp God's word and can apply it in practical life and discipling. Usually this is best done in Bible school or seminary. Discipling programs like Navigators or Campus Crusade for Christ develop adequate skills and knowledge for certain ministry roles.

Another factor in determining appropriate Bible

training is national church expectations or visa requirements. For instance, Taiwan requires anyone coming to that country on a missionary visa a minimum of two years of secular work experience, two years of theological training and two years full-time Christian work experience. Actually, it's helpful criteria for any potential missionary.

Generally speaking, anyone going into pioneer church planting needs the kind of Bible and church ministry training which a Master of Divinity would best provide. A number of schools now offer special degree programs for the would-be cross-cultural missionary. Studies in missiology deal with areas of church growth, cross-cultural communication, anthropology, contextualization and area studies in different parts of the world.

One last critical element relates to spiritual warfare and power encounters. In recent years there has been a welcomed re-emphasis on the spiritual nature of ministry. Encounters with the demonic are inevitable when bringing the gospel to people steeped in spiritual bondage and non-Christian worldviews. Have you seen God answer prayer in the face of opposition? Are you ready to do spiritual battle and know how to use your spiritual weapons (Eph. 6)?

4. **Exposure to other cultures.** A missionary is essen-

tially dealing with culture. Inappropriate approaches in cultures where the gospel is perceived as irrelevant and unintelligible almost always end in failure.

Therefore, it is extremely beneficial for anyone working overseas to have some cross-cultural exposure before going, in addition to cross-cultural studies. Short-term or summer programs offer exposure to another culture. At the same time, opportunities abound within our international communities for cross-cultural experience. Soaking yourself in the ethnic community of interest will give you a good idea of how they think. A critical part of this training is in your own attitudes and responses to cultural differences and world views. Ethnocentrism (seeing your own culture as the only right way) plagues all of us to a certain degree, but unnoticed and unchecked will destroy the effectiveness of a missionary. Exposure to cultural differences here help in preparing you for effective cross-cultural ministry.

5. **Development of relational and communication skills.** Ultimately, a missionary is only as effective as his or her ability to relate and communicate. Can you work in a team? Can you reach out and befriend people? Do you speak or teach in ways people clearly understand? Some of these skills come through formal training, but honest feedback with periodic evaluations by mentors in a local church setting can

help significantly. The bottom line is, if you can't make friends and work well with people in your own country, it isn't going to happen 10,000 miles away. If communicating in English is difficult, you will have serious problems trying it through Urdu, Cantonese or Tagalog, plus cultural barriers.

MAJORING ON THE MAJORS

In looking at the needs of the world, the greatest challenge to missions is evangelizing the 11,000 unreached people groups. Working with existing churches in training and discipling is important and may lead to mobilizing them for further outreach. The goal of missions is to lay foundations where there are none; to pioneer places where the gospel is unknown.

What was Paul's basic strategy as a missionary in Romans 15:17-22?

_____

_____

_____

_____

In calling for the thousands of pioneer church planters still needed, we often encounter a problem. Many young people can't see themselves as a church planter. The term alone puts off some because it's outside their experience. The task sounds highly ominous, like qualifying as a brain surgeon or astronaut. Essentially, church planting involves a cluster of skills most of us can develop. Cliff Bedell, professor of missions at Columbia International University, devised a helpful "skill-quiz" to indicate your potential in church planting and direct you in strengthening or developing necessary skills.

CHURCH-PLANTING SKILL QUIZ

Circle: Yes, No or Unsure

1.   Am I friendly and relaxed with an individual or small group of people I've not met before?
     Yes   No   Unsure
2.   Can I start a conversation with a stranger?
     Yes   No   Unsure
3.   Can I explain to someone good reasons for studying the Bible?
     Yes   No   Unsure
4.   Can I ask neighbors to join me in a Bible study?
     Yes   No   Unsure
5.   I can teach a series on John's Gospel explaining salvation.
     Yes   No   Unsure
6.   Can I share my own experience in becoming a Christian?
     Yes   No   Unsure
7.   Can I answer simple questions on becoming a Christian?
     Yes   No   Unsure

8. Can I get people to tell me what they are learning in my Bible study group?

Yes   No   Unsure

9. Can I teach new believer how to pray?

Yes   No   Unsure

10. Can I invite people to a Bible study in another's home.

Yes   No   Unsure

11. Can I delegate to faithful attendees simple responsibilities within a Bible study group?

Yes   No   Unsure

12. Do I know how to labor in prayer for spiritual enlightenment and growth for the members of my Bible class?

Yes   No   Unsure

13. Can I teach new believers the basics of the Christian life?

Yes   No   Unsure

14. Can I objectively discuss a problem with members of a small group and help them come to a decision without imposing my will?

Yes   No   Unsure

15. Can I teach someone else to teach a Bible lesson?

Yes   No   Unsure

16. Could I let another prepared class member teach the class?

Yes   No   Unsure

17. Can I shift the decision making dynamic from

myself to the small group or group leaders?

Yes   No   Unsure

18. Can I encourage another person, or group of people to be faithful in serving the Lord?

Yes   No   Unsure

19. Can I help a group find ways of starting new Bible studies elsewhere?

Yes   No   Unsure

20. Can I train them to share their faith with others?

Yes   No   Unsure

Well, how did you do? Evaluate your skill level by giving yourself 5 points for every yes reply, and 3 points for every answer of which you are unsure. If you scored 70 points or above, it's likely you already have many of the basic skills for pioneer church planting. If you scored relatively low, you have some idea of what's needed to prepare.

At the same time, no one is required to have every spiritual gift. We are asked to develop what we have been given (1 Peter 4:10-11), and be willing to use it in complement with the Body of Christ.

Most of us fear the unknown and failure. If we begin with basic skills and focus on developing them, other things will fall into place. God can prepare you to be an effective church planter or cross-cultural missionary. Let me close this chapter with a dialogue on church planting by Cliff Bedell. I think you'll get the application.

A: Are you an apple tree planter?

B: No! As a matter of fact I have never planted an apple tree in my life!

A: Don't you think you might be an apple tree planter anyway?

B: No, I already told you that I have never done that sort of thing.

A: But you drive a pickup truck?

B: Yes, of course! What a question!

A: And can you locate a nursery in the yellow pages of the telephone directory?

B: Sure! I let my fingers do the walking!

A: And do you think you can drive out there and pick up an apple tree with its roots tied up in sacking?

B: Sure!

A: And can you deliver that tree to another address, dig a hole big enough to contain the balled roots, and drop the apple tree in it?

B: This is getting ridiculous; sure, I can do that.

A: And can you put the dirt back in the hole and soak the surrounding ground thoroughly with water?

B: No problem.

A: I thought you told me you weren't an apple tree planter?

Write out your reaction to the above dialogue. How can you apply it in your own life?

_____

_____

_____

_____

_____

_____

_____

_____

Perhaps it's obvious by now that you're not cut out to
be a church planter. Your circumstances or gifts deter
you from going. What can you do with the Great
Commission?

_____

_____

_____

12

keeping a
world vision

It's not just starting a race that counts, but how well we finish. That was often in my mind in the early stages of missionary preparation and later field service. It's easy to get excited about something new, but difficult to maintain interest when the glamour fades and the mundane settles in.

What about yourself? How do you pursue your vision and faithfully accomplish all that God purposes for your life! In this closing chapter, I want to focus on the twin issues of persistence and staying power.

Look at Luke 9:57-62. What was the basic command of Jesus?

_____

_____

_____

_____

How were potential followers distracted?

_____

_____

_____

_____

How do we stay on track?

_____

_____

_____

_____

Again in Luke 14:25-33 Jesus rehearses the cost of being a true disciple. What vital elements are demanded?

_____

_____

_____

_____

Please remember faithfulness and obedience are costly. Whenever we commit ourselves to a fresh act of obedience, we will likely be tested in that commitment. Read the story of the disciples in the storm from Mark 4:35-41. What quality had Jesus being trying to teach his disciples earlier in the chapter?

_____

_____

What is the significance of this severe trial just after the important lessons Jesus had conveyed?

_____

_____

_____

_____

Is there a possible parallel for yourself at this stage in your commitment to be, do or go wherever the Lord should direct? Should these testings be considered positive or negative feedback on our commitments?

_____

_____

_____

_____

There is many a slip between the call and the plane for missionaries these days. Let's rehearse some of the possible obstacles or diversions ahead to warn against distraction and encourage ourselves in persistence.

OBSTACLES TO GOING

In spite of the massive amounts of mission information available to Christians today, few actually make it to the field. Most mission societies have lists of personnel needs begging to be filled. In addition, missionaries of the "great generation" that surged into missions following World War 2 are now retiring. The gaps left in the ranks overseas are frightening. Why is it so difficult to fill their places and build teams for penetrating new fields? If the command to go and make disciples of every ethnic group is still valid, and the needs remain unmet, what is hindering us from taking the challenge?

Obstacle 1—Confusion of Task

Confusion stalls many of us. The church of Jesus Christ has become a worldwide phenomena, and for that we praise God. The messages from international Christians, or reports you read, say the church is strong elsewhere. It's easy to conclude missionaries are not really needed. The job is done and the option closed.

Reports of great growth don't mean the task is finished. We need to keep in mind something mentioned in Chapter 11. Although close to 30 percent of the world's population professes allegiance to some kind of Christianity, huge pockets of unmet needs exist. An estimated 11,000 people groups are waiting to be reached. These people represent the highest priority for missions, and until they are adequately reached, it's far too early to talk about staying home.

In light of the above, can you identify places in the world where you feel missionaries are urgently needed?

_____

_____

_____

What countries or regions represent the greatest needs?

_____

_____

_____

_____

What can you do to correct the misconception that the missionary task is done?

_____

_____

_____

Obstacle 2—Professional Suicide

How frequently one hears the remark from well-trained Christian workers, "I don't want to go where I can't use my training." While legitimate from the standpoint of biblical stewardship, this excuse often masks a fear of professional suicide. In other words, many feel a pioneer mission field would not hold the scope and challenge, or ministry resources, to adequately use their professional skills and experience.

How would you respond to this challenge?

_____

_____

_____

_____

_____

This fear is frequently based on an inadequate understanding of the demands of cross-cultural church planting and church nurture. Missions is not a "losers occupation." Past generations of Christians sent the best to foreign shores because they realized the tremendous demands and skills required. No less than the best is needed today.

In all fairness, it should be said that some aspects of your training will not have equal transfer value. This is true in all of life. Thousands of people make mid-career vocational changes every year. With the demands of today's job market, it's actually the exceptional university graduate who stays exclusively in the field of his training.

How did Jesus view Peter's fishing abilities and vocational experience in determining how he would serve the kingdom in Mark 1:16-20?

_____

_____

_____

I'm convinced God will not waste your training and background if your life is totally yielded to him. The bottom line of missionary involvement is not your training and professional experience, but your availability. God wants *you* first; the skills he has given you are secondary in comparison.

Obstacle 3—Family Considerations

The welfare of the Christian family is rightfully under scrutiny. The general deterioration of family solidarity and traditional values make it a necessity for Christians to build a family life consistent with biblical principles.

Is it feasible to fulfill your responsibilities as a missionary and the needs of your family at the same time? What potential conflicts do you see?

_____

_____

_____

_____

No one takes a family into a place of potential danger, hardship and separation from the "normal" lifestyle lightly. Is it right for us to ignore the Great Commission because of the inherent dangers or problems? Look at Matthew 10:37-39 for a response.

_____

_____

_____

_____

_____

Unfortunately, some young families are turned off to missions by distorted information. While raising and educating a family overseas is a challenge, it is by no means an impossible task. Recent studies on the effects of cross-cultural living and separation for schooling, indicate missionary kids can survive and even thrive in that environment.

If you are single but hoping that God will lead a life partner your way, you needn't compromise your goals for marital security. God is well able to meet your needs as a single missionary. Unfortunately too many people have been sidetracked from God's best by marriage to a person unwilling or unable to go overseas.

Obstacle 4—The Deputation Gauntlet

Missionary support is a real obstacle. The idea of extensive travel and selling yourself as a useful product to a reluctant missions committee could scare anyone. Many are uncomfortable "tooting their own horn." Dependence on other Christians and having no control of one's welfare is enough to keep some people from considering missions.

How did Paul view support for Christian workers in 1 Corinthians 9:7-14?

_____

_____

_____

_____

_____

Deputation needn't be the horrible ordeal many imagine. To begin with, accepting support for the sake of the gospel is not demeaning. In fact, interdependence is a biblical desirable. In some cases it's necessary (1 Cor. 9:14). Deputation is a time to share one's God-given ministry with others so they can intelligently pray and participate in it. It should be seen as a ministry to churches. Deputation in proper form keeps Christians from forgetting the Great Commission and models the committed life in flesh and blood. The Apostle Paul saw the enlistment of others in his ministry (and missions in general) as an important and necessary task (Rom. 15:23-33).

What kind of person is needed for this kind of effective deputation ministry?

_____

_____

_____

_____

How can you prepare yourself for that ministry?

_____

_____

_____

_____

_____

What can you do to guard against using the obstacles mentioned as excuses for quitting?

_____

_____

_____

_____

STEPS TO THE MISSION FIELD

Simple formulas in the Christian life are best avoided. However, there are some basic steps which, if taken, can help you reach the right destination. The following steps are designed to help you maintain your vision and stay on the right track.

1. **Pray daily for mission concerns.** The best way to keep your vision burning bright is to be prayerfully involved with what God is doing world-wide. As a missionary your vision is imperative. How often do you pray for world missions now? How are you cultivating this ministry in your own life?

    _____

    _____

    _____

    _____

2. **Read one or more books about world missions.** As was mentioned before, there are excellent resource books on missions and a plethora of mis-

sionary biographies to stimulate and challenge you. One resource book I strongly recommend is *In the Gap: What it Means to be a World Christian* by David Bryant of InterVarsity. What book have you selected? Have you started reading it yet?

_____

_____

3. **Support a missionary financially or share in a missions project.** Jesus said that where your treasure is, there would be your heart also. Are you giving to missions now?

    _____

4. **Stay available.** Are you really open to whatever God may have for you and willing to do it?

    _____

    _____

5. **Investigate what's happening.** This involves basic fact-finding of needs and opportunities. God does not usually guide us in a vacuum. The needs of the world are overwhelming, and you can only do one job at a time. Knowing the needs and opportunities directs you to the needs you can best meet. There is no shortage of data available about programs, needs and procedures for becoming a missionary. Avail yourself of this information and look careful-

ly and prayerfully at the facts. Have you checked with your church leadership or missions committee about their goals for missions or priority needs?

_____

_____

6. **Keep involved.** Another important step in determining your place in missions is to be involved in ministry now. Exercise your spiritual gifts and participate in ministries within and outside the local church. Get a realistic assessment of your strengths, weaknesses and ways in which the Lord would use you. What ministries are you involved in now?

_____

_____

_____

7. **Consult godly leadership.** Not only is your personal sense of guidance important, but also the assessment of godly people around you. Consult with your church leaders and pastor. Do they share the same sense of guidance about your suitability?

_____

_____

Do they sense you are ready and prepared?

_____

8. **Prepare for what's ahead.** A call to ministry is also a call to preparation. Instead of asking what is the least you need to do before going abroad, ask what is the best preparation possible, so you can be maximally effective. Perseverance in a race means twice as much when the desire is to win and not just finish.

9. **Pray for guidance.** It is no vain thing to wait quietly on the Lord. God has promised to lead the believer, so we can depend on him to make the way clear. Are you praying regularly for God's direction in your life? What should you be asking him?

    _____

    _____

10. **Make application when the time is right.** Besides learning the needs and opportunities, you need to know the mission agencies your church endorses or recommends. The agency desires early contact so they can know you and have a part in your training and preparation. The mission will also value close contact with your home church to work together in application, appointment and final departure to the field. Have you become familiar with the application procedures of several likely mission agencies?

_____

_____

11. **Be commissioned by your church.** I am convinced biblically that missionaries should not just go, but be sent! God desires a partnership between the sending church and mission agency. The endorsement, recognition of suitability and gifts, and committed support in prayer and finance from the church is invaluable to any would-be missionary. How does your church demonstrate this kind of partnership?

_____

_____

_____

A FINAL WORD

Sometimes the road to missionary service seems endless, filled with obstacles and truly difficult to walk. Many have started, but have lost the vision or been sidetracked because of "better" offers or more comfortable terms at home. You must count the costs realistically.

At the same time, some simple facts must be kept before us which ultimately determine our choices. The first is God's command to go and make disciples of every nation. It is not a question of whether or not I should participate in the Great Commission, but how and where. The Book commands me, and obedience is not optional.

The second fact is the world's needs. As we have already seen most of the world's inhabitants are unreached. Asia, for instance, represents two-thirds of the human race, but only five percent of the world's Christians.

The third fact to be kept central in our thinking is the divine enablement promised for discipling the nations. The scope of our mandate is absolutely overwhelming and we feel like spiritual pygmies before all the giants of the world. But Jesus himself said with all the authority of heaven, "And surely I am with you always, to the very end of the age." Divine presence and power for the task are promised us, no matter where we are called to serve.

What can we say to the student at the missions conference who questioned, "If God is calling, why is he so hard to hear?" Is it really so difficult to know whether God is calling you or your neighbor into missions? Ultimately, the problem lies not with God but with us on this end. Isn't our real difficulty a problem in hearing, or even in willingness to listen? Unfortunately most Christians don't even ask the question, "Am I called?"

I am convinced that God is trustworthy and willing and able to guide his child. The Lord of the Harvest hasn't left the task of finding our individual fields of service to blind guesswork. If we weren't preoccupied with other things, hard-hearted or self-centered, the issue wouldn't seem so complicated. If the Great Commission is still valid today, then many more must respond to God's call than are doing so now. We have the guidelines of Scripture and the promise of the Holy Spirit's guidance. Never before have we had so much technology and support structures to do the job.

The last fact to consider is the question of my willingness to obey the command of Christ, see the need, appropriate the resources and be a part of God's work in this world. Without that willingness everything else is academic and meaningless. As we said before, God looks for availability first, rather than mere ability. It isn't our wisdom he seeks but our willingness. By completing this course you've proven your interest. Now, can you offer him your willingness?

appendix — missions as a second career

O ne of the encouraging trends in recent years has been the dramatic increase in hands-on missions involvement by retirees or those taking up missions as a second career. Some have retired early to specifically start a new career in missions, others have begun investigating the opportunities as retirement began. In the United States these people are sometimes known as "finishers" (*www.finishers.org*). Here is a brief introduction to some of the roles finishers may be involved in, and a look at some things to keep in mind when considering serving as a finisher in missions.

For someone with a passion for God's glory, a servant's heart and flexible attitude, the opportunities for involvement in missions are vast! These can range from indirect support ministries to direct involvement in cross-cultural evangelism, discipleship and church planting. A one- to three-year period for involvement is common, not counting the many two- to four-week opportunities available. And of course, there are some avenues of service that could last for many years.

Depending on your experience and the need for learning a new language, there are often opportunities for retirees in "frontline" ministries, even in evangelism, discipleship and church planting. Even without the local language, there may be an opportunity to be a part of a team teaching a foreign language such as English. This can make a strategic contribution to a church-planting team's efforts to meet a felt need and make new contacts, and can be a great avenue to making and developing friendships.

Other opportunities could involve a role in Bible translation, student outreach, children's ministries, economic development outreach projects, medical services, church facilities development, humanitarian relief and micro-enterprise development. And while it doesn't necessarily involve leaving your home country, taking an active role in missions mobilization could be the kind of strategic opportunity that would allow you to multiply yourself into many unreached people groups.

"Behind the scenes" or support ministry opportunities could include caring for children of missionaries in home schooling and dormitory environments; teaching in a school specializing in the education of the children of missionaries; working in an administrative center with finances (bookkeepers and accountants are in high demand), computer/IT training and support, personnel management; serving as host or hostess at a mission home or training center; and "team grandparenting"—some church-planting teams would love to have someone who is savvy, with "real life" experience (including parenting) to come alongside as life and ministry mentors. Most mission agencies will not have this as an official job description, but church, agency or other relationships may lead you to such an opportunity. These are just some of the many avenues to make a meaningful contribution through some kind of support ministry.

Here are some things to remember as you are thinking and praying through a more hands-on involvement in missions as a finisher.

1. Serving cross-culturally for a length of time can be physically, emotionally and spiritually demanding. Many of the observations in this book about preparation for the mission field hold true whether it is for a one-year commitment or a ten-year one.

2. If you work with an organization such as a missions agency, the way they operate overseas may be closer to the host culture than the one you know them in. Sometimes this leads to "culture shock" with the organization.

3. It is vitally important to have a team of prayer partners standing with you, whether you are doing bookkeeping or church planting.

4. Finally, many finishers try to go totally self-funded. While we would not necessarily discourage that, there are two things to remember: missionaries should be "sent" by their local church—this is not something that someone should just do on their own, whether they need the money or not. Second, remember that the financial involvement of others in the ministry to which God sends you is a biblical model. Paul talks about it in 2 Corinthians. Prayerfully consider chapters 8 and 9 as you decide how to finance your involvement in missions, and read some of the excellent books on support development.

about the author

Dr. Daniel W. Bacon is a graduate of Dallas Theological Seminary and has a D.Miss. from Trinity Evangelical Divinity School. He and his wife Lindie were church-planting missionaries in Japan with OMF International (formerly the China Inland Mission) for ten years. From 1978 to 1998 he served as the U.S. Director for OMF. He was also OMF's International Director for Mobilization, and is now the Director for Member Development for OMF world-wide.